How Your Family Can Flourish

How Your Family Can Flourish

*A Guide to
Christian Living
in a
Post-Christian
Culture*

Ray E. Ballmann

CROSSWAY BOOKS • WHEATON, ILLINOIS
A DIVISION OF GOOD NEWS PUBLISHERS

How Your Family Can Flourish.

Copyright © 1991 by Ray E. Ballmann.

Published by Crossway Books, a division of
Good News Publishers, 1300 Crescent Street, Wheaton, Illinois 60187.

All rights reserved. No part of this publication may be reproduced, stored in a retrieval system or transmitted in any form by any means, electronic, mechanical, photocopy, recording or otherwise, without the prior permission of the publisher, except as provided by USA copyright law.

Cover design: Russ Peterson

First printing, 1991

Printed in the United States of America

Unless otherwise noted, all Bible quotations are taken from *Holy Bible: New International Version*, copyright © 1978 by the New York International Bible Society. Used by permission of Zondervan Bible Publishers.

Library of Congress Cataloging-in-Publication Data
Ballman, Ray E.
   How your family can flourish : a guide to Christian living in a post-Christian culture / Ray E. Ballman.
      p.   cm.
   Includes bibliographical references and index.
   1. Family—Religious life.   I. Title.
BV4526.2B355   1991   248.4—dc20   91-3836
ISBN 0-89107-628-X

99	98	97	96	95	94	93	92	91
15	14	13	12	11	10	9	8	7	6	5	4	3	2	1

To my beloved wife, Cindy,
for her encouragement, patience,
and understanding

To Jan Dennis and Ted Griffin,
for their godly advice and keen insight

To all Christian parents
seeking to make an impact on the
world in which they live

TABLE OF CONTENTS

Introduction   ix
1 The Challenge to Christian Families   11
2 Assaults on the Family, Part I   19
3 Assaults on the Family, Part II   35
4 Families Following the Master   45
5 Faithful in a Fallen Culture   51
6 Radical Christian Living, Part I   77
7 Radical Christian Living, Part II   91
8 Radical Christian Living, Part III   103
9 Radical Christian Living, Part IV   117
10 What? My Family Missionaries?   129
11 Mission Options for Your Family   145
12 Conclusion: The Essence of a Flourishing Family   163

Appendix A: Home Education Resources   167

Appendix B: Scheduling a Life-changing Seminar in Your Area: "Building an Effective Family Life!"   171

Appendix C: Short-term Mission Opportunities   173

Appendix D: Charts on Factors Impacting Family Life   193

Appendix E: Guiding Principles of Flourishing Family Life   199

Notes   203

Scripture Index   209

General Index   213

INTRODUCTION

Strong families are the foundation of society. Through them we pass on our traditions, rituals, and values. From them we receive the love, encouragement, and education needed to meet human challenges. (Former President Ronald Reagan)

Christians everywhere are looking for answers to strengthen and bolster their family unity. This is not a superficial book on "how to have a perfect family," nor one that glosses over the real problems families face. We have too often seen Band-aids and elixirs used when surgery was required. Rather, it shares tough solutions conceived out of a desperate need for a new approach and born out of years of personal experience and a desire to see families flourish. This is not intended to be light reading on the family, but a book that presents radical answers for the radical problems Christian families are encountering today.

In my years of counseling Christian families, I have observed a growing inconsistency between the goals and real experience of Christian people. Many parents in my counseling room have poured out their heart's desire for a close-knit family. These men and women are active in the church and sincere in their faith, yet lack a rich measure of family harmony and witness. The majority of these families were experiencing in their homes unnecessary marital distress, rebellious teenagers, sexual impropriety, and twisted priorities—problems no different than their non-Christian counterparts. Many of these problems could have been prevented if radical Christian procedures had earlier been implemented.

Are you seeking to improve interpersonal relationships in your family? Do you sincerely desire deeper marital communication? Do you yearn for respectful children that treasure their time with you above all else? Do you want a family experience that is markedly different from that of the world? Do you desire to leave behind you the legacy of a godly heritage? Let's explore an exciting approach to family living.

ONE

The Challenge to Christian Families

Jan is a sweet, young girl from a typical, conservative Christian home. She is the middle child of three and attends a local Christian high school in suburban California. Her parents are kindhearted and emotionally stable. Yet at sweet sixteen she isn't so innocent. She is hooked on drugs and immoral parties. Her attitudes have little by little drifted away from that of her parents, and she handles life in a radically different way than she was taught as a child. Massive emotional trauma and heartache come to the stunned parents as they make the shocking discovery. They lie awake at nights crying on each other's shoulders. Over and over they ask, "Where did we go wrong?"

There was no abuse in the home. By Jan's own admission she received plenty of attention from her parents and the rest of the family. So how did this happen?

It all started when Jan began to circulate with certain friends who adversely affected her value formation. The parents, on their part, failed to recognize what children and teens are like today, even those who call themselves Christians.

Fortunately, this story has a good ending, though many do not. Jan sought help at New Horizons, a school in the Dominican Republic especially designed to help teens deal with attitudinal problems and peer pressure. Through cultural separation, hard work, and intensive Christian counseling, Jan was able to get back on track.

It's wonderful that there are Christian ministries to help wayward teenagers or help rebuild broken families, but it is better yet to avoid such situations. How can we keep ourselves and our children from unsuspectingly going astray in a world determined to bring us down?

Christians are generally aware that families are under dire satanic attack in these trying days. Our families today face a society saturated with humanism and selfishness, rampant sexual immorality, liberal media bias, a culture with growing anti-family attitudes, and the shouldering of a disproportionate tax burden.[1]

Youngsters too have a heavy load to bear. They face a country saddled with enormous debt and social problems, societal images that assign a new definition to morality, relentless peer pressure that diminishes self-respect, individuality, and creativity, and public classrooms that spawn alienation from and rebellion toward parents. With the loss of pro-family sentiment in the wider culture, it is small wonder America has such a staggering number of Humpty-Dumpty families.

CHANGING CULTURAL ATTITUDES TOWARD THE FAMILY

Lack of radical Christian convictions and lifestyle combined with cultural coercion has led many Christian families into a state of tragic compromise. The attitudes of our society have permeated Christian family life, and thus the Christian family has lost its harmony and spiritual power.

Twenty-five years ago pro-abortion activists were fighting for national legalization, day-care centers were rare, the father was considered the unquestioned head of the home, families were less fragmented by divorce and in-house abuse, and AIDS was unheard of. While we cannot turn back the clock, we can respond in a hard-hitting and intelligent way to save our dear families. Many parents earnestly desire to follow a family lifestyle that produces rich fulfillment, satisfaction, and enduring reward, but only radical Christian family living will cause families to flourish. This is a formidable undertaking! For the family striving to stay faithful to God and consecrated to Christ in a value-adulterated culture, there are no easy answers. We must make some difficult decisions based on sound judgment informed by Biblical teaching.

Christian family values are easily entangled in webs of prevalent societal lifestyles. Thus in this opening chapter we will examine a few of the key issues facing families today. Unless we know what the problems of the nineties are, it is impossible to adequately confront them. Unless we understand the strategies of the enemy, we cannot resist his attacks. In these opening pages I will not attempt to offer in-depth solutions, but will draw a broad overview of the cultural sources of value contamination. A comprehensive solution will be laid out later in the book.

MODEL EROSION

Model erosion among husbands, wives, and children assaults the modern family from a number of areas. Television, movies, videos, and textbooks have redefined the role of modern-day family members. The aftermath of the women's liberation movement has changed our society's concept of the family and its structure. The radical feminist movement of the sixties advocated among other things the repudiation of the traditional feminine role model. This started with protest rallies, the symbolic burning of female undergarments, "choice" advocacy, and the supposed right to be equal with men in every way. At first society scoffed and looked down upon such rhetoric and demonstrations as extremist and fanatical. However, over the years untiring persistence has paid off: feminist thinking has infiltrated every aspect of society and law.

The Equal Rights Amendment did not become a constitutional reality, but radical feminist rights have by stealth entered the mainstream of American society. Some of the chief conquests of proponents of this view include: abortion-on-demand, massive entry of women into the work force, "comparable worth," a federal baby-sitting act, and the feminization of the U.S. armed forces and military academies. (In 1989 a 112-pound, 5'4", straggly-haired twenty-year-old girl was chosen to be first captain of the Corps of Cadets, West Points' highest honor, putting her in charge of overseeing virtually all aspects of life for 4,400 Academy cadets.) Have these changes strengthened or weakened our country's moral fabric? From the standpoint of Biblical truth, we would have to say the latter.

Modern culture has saturated us with the idea that the roles of men and women, husbands and wives, fathers and mothers are interchangeable. Consequently, many husbands have in principle abdicated their responsibility as the fundamental breadwinner for the family, actually encouraging their wives to seek employment outside the home. Guilt trips are laid at their wives' feet, convincing them their families cannot survive financially without two incomes. Similarly, some insist that the wife make a financial contribution to the family budget. While this may be necessary in a few households, it is frequently merely a convenient excuse to support a more affluent or self-indulgent lifestyle. The man may feel his arguments are justified, but the consequences are often bitter.

Furthermore, many husbands no longer envision their primary calling as spiritual head of the family. Shirking this responsibility produces a domino affect resulting in chaotic family conditions. Many men relying on the flesh become overly concerned about material accumulation, retirement security, or sports or personal recreation, all to the detriment of their greatest treasure: *their families*. Under these conditions men become less and less effective as husbands and fathers.

For example, some get more upset about a scratch on their car or the new furniture than about blocked marital communication. Some are more concerned about missing "Monday Night Football" than about missing an opportunity to read to or pray with their children. Some work harder and put more time, planning, and thought into building their earthly empire or retirement plan than into building a spiritual legacy. The results can be ruinous. Every father ought to ask himself, "Whose drum am I training my children to march to? Am I raising my children for God or for the god of this world?" When fathers relinquish spiritual headship, the family is vulnerable to structural breakdown.

Mothers also frequently compromise their motherhood, sometimes in an attempt to pick up the reins of leadership their husbands have neglected. The liberalization of women's role and function in society has resulted in some good for women, but it has also brought great burdens upon home life. In fact, it has brought more harm than good. A fire is great to cook with—unless it oversteps its boundaries and burns down the home.

Many mothers with small children have been led to believe there is no self-fulfillment without pursuing their own careers, as though mothering is not a satisfying or honorable career in itself. Gone are the days when the American female majority cherishes an exclusive role as wife, mother, and homemaker. Rebellious feminists have cast a pejorative light on these traditional roles, describing them as lowly, provincial, humiliating, and detestable. Today over 60 percent of women work outside the home.

But women's storming into the work force has left its indelible mark: homemaking has taken a backseat to career, children are being forced into day-care centers or have been doomed to become latch-key children, husbands have lost their self-esteem as sole providers and breadwinners, unemployment has grown as men are edged out of potential jobs, and family time has been overshadowed by relaxation time in front of the television set since the evening leaves both Mommy and Daddy tired and worn-out.

Today it is extremely difficult to find a neighborhood where the majority of mothers remain home during the day. Delivery men frequently go house to house searching for an occupied home where they can leave a parcel. Many churches find it hard to have a well-attended, mid-morning women's Bible study or prayer meeting since only a handful are available for attendance. Ironically, evangelical church-sponsored day-care centers are teeming with small, homesick children forced to be separated from Mom daily.

Observing the unfavorable examples provided by many moms and dads, children have become role-confused. Hence, children too become confused about their God-ordained roles and rebel against the divine order. This manifests itself in vigorous resistance to parental authority and appropriate submission. Their minds implode due to the constant flood of societally redefined images of family roles. Younger and younger ages are being exposed to an early sexual consciousness. Like tape recorders that never stop, their impressionable minds are constantly picking up everything from the cultural role models that surround them, especially those on TV. Gone are the nostalgic days of such television shows as "Father Knows Best," "Leave It to Beaver," "Make Room for Daddy," "Hazel," etc. in which traditional role models were heralded. In recent years shows such as "Cagney and Lacey," "Moonlighting"—these first being classic examples of the female careerist mentality, "Thirtysomething," "The Simpsons," "Married with Children," and many others mock traditional family values. Most modern productions go well out of their way to exemplify role reversal in the family. Such is the society in which we live.

Guiding Principle:

A successful family is one which places its home under the authority of Jesus Christ, in which the husband is the head of the home and loves his wife as Christ loves the church, in which the wife is both helpmeet and homemaker, submitting to her husband as to the Lord, and in which the children are obedient to both. This is the God-given model.

A FAMINE OF FAMILY TOGETHERNESS

Improper time priorities is another culturally inspired nemesis of family life. An old adage states, "Nothing good comes easy." Though not all homespun wisdom is true, it is hard to question the veracity of this statement. Great works of art are not painted in a few moments, exquisite furniture requires much time at the hand of a master craftsman, and *there are no shortcuts in developing quality family relationships!* Families flourish under a *quantitative* and *qualitative* time investment on the part of a loving couple.

It is sometimes said that quantity time is not necessary as long as you give quality time. This is not so. Many people give their spouse or children token time, but the consequences speak for themselves. *Quality relationships require quantity time investment!* Suppose you need a triple heart bypass operation, and the doctor says, "I can have you in and out of the operating room in five minutes." That kind of talk wouldn't inspire much confidence. You might ask, "What is your success ratio?" The doctor says, "Don't worry about it. I've got my technique down to a rapid art. I can cut, repair, and close in five minutes, and I do nothing but quality work." If you're like me, you would seek another surgeon immediately. Common sense and good judgment tell you a physician can perform major surgery just so fast and still have safety and success. The same is true of family life.

Fallacious counsel is freely offered by many who themselves do not understand the concept of true family. To all who would give you such advice you must ask yourself, "What is *their* family life like?" Some offer marital advice while the ruins of their marriage and family lie smoldering in the background.

Like a house of cards, many families are susceptible to falling apart at the smallest disturbance because they are missing one of the essentials of stable family life—*spending time together*. The facts speak for themselves. A recent survey shows that an average working American couple spends four minutes a day in meaningful conversation. More ominous still, that same couple only spends thirty seconds a day in meaningful conversation *with their children*.[2] Another study involving 2,400 fifth-graders revealed that the thing that upset these children most was spending too little time with their parents.[3] With so many things going on—personal pursuits, television, sports, hobbies, club meetings, even church meetings—many families have precious little time left over for building relationships. Giving the family your leftover time after personal recreation and television viewing is simply not good enough.

The reason frequently given for not spending more time with the family is "busyness." It is true that work occupies a good portion of a person's waking hours, but the need for employment is common to all households. Unless you are self-employed, it is a block of time which is beyond your control—predetermined time. The critical difference comes in how a family spends time that is *not* predetermined, elective time. This includes weeknights, weekends, vacations, holidays, and any time not required for essential income production. Busyness can so easily crowd out family time and family participation. But a wrong choice here will exact a price on the family.

Some years back Harry Chapin wrote a song entitled "The Cat's in the Cradle." The lyrics depicted a father who had no time to spend with his son because he was too busy making a living. The song concluded with the son as a grown man and the father desiring to spend time with him. Now the shoe is on the other foot, and the son is too busy to spend time with his father. The moral of the song was, the son had grown up just like his father.

It is so easy to retort "Later" or "Not right now, I'm too busy" or "We'll do it when I get time." Too often that time never comes. The days turn into weeks, the weeks into months, and the months into years. Before you know it, the opportunity is gone or the promise forgotten. It doesn't take long before the children are grown and gone. We must *make time*, we must *plan time*, or the time will never come.

Guiding Principle:

Each of us has enough time to do what we were placed here to do. That must be our central focus—to work earnestly in fulfilling the purpose the Master has for us. Time efficiency will elude us as long as Jesus is not sitting on the throne of highest priority in our hearts.

TWO
Assaults on the Family, Part I

PUBLIC EDUCATION— PORTRAIT OF ACADEMIC FAILURE

Imagine that your state enacts legislation requiring your child to enroll in a series of government-sponsored swimming classes. Swimming is an important skill to master, so you have no objections. Instruction is given daily for twelve consecutive summers, and you are promised tremendous results. The lessons are supported by the taxpayers at a considerable rate. You tolerate the taxation since your child, it is promised, will learn the fine art of swimming. The taxes also generate enough revenue to provide the finest swimming facilities in the world.

Several months after classes begin, you ask your child to demonstrate what he has learned. You find out that your child has developed an intense fear of the water and a hatred of the classes themselves. The instructor tells you this is natural and will pass with time. The next year you again ask your child to demonstrate what he has learned. He reluctantly lowers himself into the water and soon begins to panic. He tries to dog paddle, but quickly abandons this basic yet unmastered technique. The teacher tells you he is a slow learner, but he will work with your son as best as he can.

Years pass by. You hear other parents remark about the swimming difficulties their children are experiencing too. You ask your son to show you how well he can swim. Your son says, "I swim as well as the other kids. Besides, my teacher says I'm doing fine." You kindly ask again, "Would you please show me?" He says, "It's none of your business." Taken back by that surly remark, you become extremely concerned. You make a surprise poolside visit of your son's class. There you observe some surprising, even bizarre things. One instructor is obviously incompetent to teach swimming; instead, he is showing the boys and girls how to use a prophylactic device. By an empty graffiti-laden pool, many of the students are simultaneously screaming obscenities and displaying rowdy behavior. Some are openly flirting near the changing rooms, while others are buying and selling drugs near the diving board. When you ask the pool director what is going on, he responds with a barrage of lame excuses. He forcefully tells you about the low pay the instructors receive and the resulting inability to attract good ones, about uncaring parents, and about insufficient funding.

This may sound like a terrible nightmare. Yet in many ways the analogy portrays modern public education quite accurately. Educating our children is one of the cornerstones of family life. But the current state of public education renders it another cultural enemy undermining the traditional family. Fortunately, many parents are wise to the educational bankruptcy in our public schools. They see the dismal academic record, declining moral climate, unbridled discipline problems, teacher incompetence, the deterioration of self-respect, peer pressure that is overwhelmingly negative, an increasing tide of teen suicide and pregnancy, chronic alcohol and drug abuse, a growing trend towards alienation from parents, textbooks that teach violence, hate, and despair, the use of value clarification techniques, the teaching of relativism, death education, and the lack of patriotism and democratic ideals. Muggings, robberies, rapes, and even murder are all a part of the picture in today's public school system.

Parents know that college entrance scores have plummeted over the last twenty years and that most schools only require one year of math and science to graduate. Dads and moms are not blind to the appalling rate of functional illiteracy in this country. Former Secretary of Education Lauro Cavazos told the American Medical Association House of Delegates that because of our twenty-seven million illiterates, "we are in danger of becoming the world's only fully industrialized Third World nation." In 1990 the National Assessment of Educational Progress compiled results of twenty years of tests which showed student performance "is low and not improving." Another conclusion which has been made is, students grasp facts but miss key concepts. In history, for example, 84 percent of eighth-graders knew how Abraham Lincoln died, but only 25 percent knew that his goal in the Civil War was to preserve the Union. Chester E. Flinn, Jr., head of the board that directed the assessment, said, "This kind of data ought to be a cold shower for the nation."[1]

Nor are parents blind to the chaos and lack of discipline in the nation's schools. Former President Ronald Reagan assessed the public school situation with these words: "Our schools are filled with rude, unruly behavior, and even violence." A telling government study entitled "Disorder in Our Public Schools" noted that in a given year 282,000 students are physically attacked on school premises, 1,000 teachers are assaulted seriously enough to require medical attention, and 125,000 teachers are threatened with bodily harm.[2] What kind of education can take place in an environment like that?

Christian parents are also concerned about public school teaching about sexuality. Because of AIDS this whole concept of sex education has gone wild, like a fire out of control. It must be remembered that innocence can never be reclaimed or reestablished. Children are not only being taught graphic details of heterosexual activity, but also homosexual activity. When he was Surgeon General, Everett Koop boldly stated, "There is now no doubt that we need sex education in schools and that it must include information on heterosexual and homosexual relationships." How sad!

A growing number of states are passing mandatory courses in which they are teaching fourth-graders, in some places even younger, in a mixed setting, how to use condoms. The devastation to modesty, decency, and purity in such a situation is horrendous. New York City school chancellor Joseph Fernandez made no secret of the fact that he wanted to distribute condoms to students in twenty junior and senior high schools, and in fact condoms are now available to students without parental knowledge or consent.[3] Many parents become livid when they find out their children are being taught explicit details of sexuality and sodomy, as well as how to use condoms.

We must also mention school-based clinics, many of which in addition to other things are providing contraceptives and family planning counseling. Currently there are approximately one hundred such clinics, with double that number in the works. SBCs are being pushed by Planned Parenthood and other self-appointed advocates of teen sexual liberation who have consistently resisted efforts to require parental consent for abortions and birth control. Once a parent signs a "blank check" consent form for his son to receive a free sports physical, the SBC has the freedom to distribute contraceptives and engage in birth control counseling without parental notification or consent.[4]

Parents know that many things are being taught in the public schools which are contrary to their own moral and religious values. Unfortunately, the problem is not only what *is* being taught but also what *is not* being taught. Godly parents believe that history, biology, English, etc. should be taught from a Christian worldview. When you have an educational setting that totally leaves God out of the picture five days a week, your child is going to have a substantial lack in his or her education. In public schools they call this academic neutrality, but in reality there is no such thing. An act is either right or wrong, and children need to be taught that. When classroom teachers instruct a class with no foundation of moral principles upon which students can make a judgment, they are creating a moral vacuum. Children in that environment will absorb whatever prevailing values are at hand, and in public schools the prevailing values are seldom Christian.

If you were charged with the hideous and unthinkable responsibility of rendering American public education ineffective, it would be difficult to create an educational Frankenstein worse than the one currently on the loose. Thousands of parents across the United States are tired of fighting an uphill battle to improve conditions in their local public schools. The academic record is a national disgrace. A reform-school environment is evidenced by a disgusting lack of discipline. Insidious, humanistic indoctrination creates doubt about one's Christian faith, while value clarification techniques foster intolerable parent/child alienation and rebellion toward parental authority. Timothy Dwight, a former president of Yale University, once said, "To commit our children to the care of irreligious persons is to commit lambs to the superintendency of wolves."

It's time to quit putting Band-aids on the hull of an academic *Titanic* and to seriously examine realistic solutions. Your son/daughter need not become another robot-like clone of academic retardation. He or she need not be condemned to mediocrity, failure and defeat.

Guiding Principle:

Parents who want their children to develop strong academic excellence, moral strength of character, and a healthy self-respect, to be socially well-adjusted, and to build spiritual depth and appreciation should seriously consider home education or a private Christian school.

CHILD CARE WITHOUT COMPASSION

Long before Margie makes the early-morning stop she makes Monday through Friday, her heart starts pounding furiously, and her palms begin to sweat. She gets a chilling feeling of guilt all over. But she has no choice—she's due at the office in thirty minutes. "Casandra," she says, fighting off the emotions of the moment, "I'll see you after I get off work. Be a good little girl for Mommy and don't cry when I leave!" They warmly embrace. Then Mom gives her precious daughter a little kiss. Casandra slowly and reluctantly opens the car door, gets out, and tearfully watches as Mom speeds off to work.

The sound and feelings are all too familiar. It's a situation repeated by millions of moms each and every workday. Parents are continually bombarded with a cultural philosophy which reinforces the economic necessity of a two-wage family. But it's time for Christian parents to be well-advised and placed on the alert! Day-care will never be able to replace the warmth of a loving home. Sometimes it is even dangerous for the child.

The number of women in the labor force has quadrupled since 1947. The infusion of young mothers in the work force has regrettably produced both latch-key children and the casual and widespread utilization of day-care centers. High on the liberal political agenda is to get Uncle Sam directly involved in the day-care industry, which will help prop up the faltering feminist cause. Feminist propaganda and the liberal media have for years consistently covered up the tragic results of day-care. Parents have been led to believe that day-care has a relatively harmless or negligible effect on children. As left-wing elements in our society promote a Pollyanna-like image of day-care, they forge ahead with this massive social experiment on children.

Instead of cautiously yielding to reliable research that does not concur with their conclusions, day-care proponents argue for building more facilities and for greater federal funding. Enter the ABC bill ("Act for Better Child Care"), sponsored by the liberal Senator Chris Dodd. The bill was designed to provide nationalized, licensed, regulated child care. Paid for by the taxpayer (cost estimates range from three to one hundred billion dollars), this law thrusts the U.S. government headfirst into the baby-sitting business. Ignoring the possible negative side effects for the children, the stubborn and self-serving defenders of day-care are more concerned about their own agenda than the well-being of children and families.

Back in 1978, child psychologists Jay Belsky and Lawrence Steinberg of Penn State University flipped on caution lights in their research paper entitled "Child Development." In this study, which highlighted the paramount need for more research on the long-term effects of day-care, they concluded,

To even say that the jury is still out on day-care would be, in our view, premature and naively optimistic. The fact of the matter is, quite frankly, that the majority of the evidence has yet to be presented, much less subpoenaed.[5]

Since that time numerous studies have emerged to show us the truth about day-care. For example, Dr. Belsky, who in 1978 had a neutral opinion on day-care, sounded an alarm in October 1985. In a paper delivered to the American Academy of Pediatrics he warned that day-care can negatively affect both the mother-child and father-child bonds. Insecure parent-child bonding, Dr. Belsky warns, can result in conduct that is characterized by "noncompliance, aggressiveness, social withdrawal, and behavior problems in general."[6] Since that time, evidence continues to mount about the negative effects of day-care.

Though day-care is culturally in vogue, intellectual honesty forces us to evaluate its many risks. Besides the weakened parental bonding already mentioned, heightened risk for disease, increased aggression, noncompliance, and emotional instability are a few of the risks of absentee motherism.

Today there are approximately one million child internees under age five in day-care centers, with another four million receiving some other type of non-maternal care. "Fully 35 percent of women with children under five are now working full-time, with another 20 percent working part-time."[7] It is appropriate to be sympathetic to mothers who have no choice but to work. However, due to the growing evidence on the adverse repercussions of institutionalizing children in day-care, the dangers must be openly discussed. I recognize that this subject can stir up an emotional hornet's nest. Yet, wise parents will want to get all the facts before using services that may have an adverse effect on their family life. The risk to victims of modern social parenting falls primarily into three areas: psychological, medical and social.

Numerous studies support a substantial correlation between strong parental bonding and *mental health*. Research conducted by child development specialist John Bowlby concluded that "the quality of the parental care which a child receives in his earliest years is of vital importance for his future mental health."[8] He further concludes that an "infant and young child should experience a *warm, intimate, and continuous relationship with his mother*"[9] (emphasis mine). Dr. Edward Levine, retired professor of social psychology at Loyola University, reported:

> Parents, especially mothers during their children's early years, are crucial in assisting their children to internalize those values that are integral for the formation of self-discipline, a sound conscience or character. If evaluated by the standard of children's mental health, *day-care is detrimental to children's emotional well-being.*"[10] (emphasis mine)

Childhood psychopathologist Dr. Humberto Nagera found in his studies that *mother-child interaction is crucial in brain development* because it increases the complexity of the pathways in the brain, promotes vascularization (making oxygen available to the organ), and favors the process of myelinization (protective sheathing of nerve fibers). Nagera's research can be supported with numerous other studies which unequivocally demonstrate the negative effects of maternal deprivation on a child's intellectual capabilities, personality, and social perception. Concluding his study, Dr. Nagera said,

> Clearly, no sensible society can afford to damage hundreds of thousands of its children by mass-producing and officially condoning, institutionalizing and supporting child-rearing practices known to produce such *disastrous results.*[11] (emphasis mine)

Based on such reliable and pragmatic research, we can surmise that routine use of day-care can place children at risk for potential psychological damage.

A whole plethora of psychological disorders can also point an accusing finger at maternal surrogatism. One of the most important of these is low self-esteem. Pediatricians, child psychologists, and educational theorists generally agree that good self-image is built and nurtured on loving and repetitive familial interaction, especially during a child's formative years. Maslow and Felker found that a sense of "belonging" is critical to a healthy self-image.[12] A recent study shows that children under eighteen months old who spend twenty or more hours a week in day-care *lose their sense of security*.[13] Further research presented at the International Conference on Infant Studies in Washington (April 22, 1988) revealed that children in full-time day-care may have poorer study skills, lower grades, diminished self-esteem, unpopularity, and uncooperative behavior by the third grade.[14] Parental proxies in a kennel-like environment will never be able to provide the large doses of custom-made love and attention children need.

There are also numerous *medical risks* endemic to day-care centers. According to researchers at the Centers for Disease Control in Atlanta, ". . . large, licensed day-care centers . . . are major transmission centers for hepatitis, severe diarrhea, and other diseases."

FACT: The Giardia parasite has been found in 29 to 54 percent of the children in various day-care centers, compared with 2 percent of age-matched children not in day-care.

FACT: Hepatitis A is a significant problem in day-care institutions across the country, according to the CDC.

FACT: Up to 22 percent of children in group day-care develop otitis media, requiring tubes to be surgically placed in the child's ears. For children in home-care, the figure is only 3 percent.

FACT: Meningitis, the infection of the membranes around the brain and/or spinal cord, is easily spread in a day-care setting. Statistically, one in ten victims die.

The diseases and acute illnesses among children in day-care settings are so prevalent that a new term has been coined by professional staffs in primary-care offices. The collective syndrome, reflecting the common source of infection, is aptly called "*Daycaritis*."[15]

Surveys indicate that up to 80 percent of children in day-care centers excrete Cytomegalovirus (CMV) in their urine and saliva. This has implications for the children's own child-bearing years later in life, as primary CMV has been unquestionably linked to serious birth defects in pregnant women. Other potential hazards to the developing infant include deafness, mental retardation, and even death. It is imperative that pregnant women with children in day-care be alerted to the perils involved.

> Writing recently in *The New England Journal of Medicine*, a team of physicians from the University of Alabama at Birmingham observed that pregnant women run "an increased risk" of contracting the potentially dangerous CMV if they have one or more children enrolled in day-care. In an earlier study the UAB team found that 59 percent of the day-care children examined were shedding CMV and that CMV was found on toys used in the day-care center. Based on antibody tests, the UAB study estimated that the cumulative infection rate among the day-care children was *between 70 and 100 percent*.[16]

There are many other medical dangers as well. Consider the following:

> *The Journal of the American Medical Association* reported a study of the disease Hemophilus Influenza Type B, a potential forerunner of childhood meningitis, epiglottis, pneumonia, arthritis, and blood and skin infections, which found that day care children were 12 times more likely to contract the disease than children cared for in the home. A Colorado study by Dr. Gregory Istre, Oklahoma's state epidemiologist, indicated that the risk doubles when children are placed in day care facilities.
>
> The chance of hepatitis breaking out in a day care center over the course of a year is between one and three percent. The risk doubles if diapered babies are present. Dr. Stephen Hadler, chief epidemiologist of the hepatitis branch for the Centers for Disease Control, stated, "Fifteen percent of all infectious hepatitis cases in the U.S. are acquired through a day care facility."

The risk of contracting diarrhea increases 30 percent when children are placed in day care centers. A study of an Atlanta facility by epidemiologists from the Centers of Disease Control found that more than 50 percent of the toddlers present were infected with a diarrhea-causing bacteria called Giardia Lambia. The rate for similar children in maternal care was two percent.[17] (emphasis mine)

According to a shocking article in the *Journal of Infectious Diseases*, a two-year study of day-care centers in Maricopa County, Arizona revealed that *of the 279 licensed centers, eighty-five or a whopping 30 percent had outbreaks of hepatitis affecting three or more families*.[18]

These frightening statistics clearly indicate that day-care facilities are viral and bacterial time bombs. After all, day-care workers can only boil the toys so often, if at all. And it's not practical to change rubber gloves after each nose wipe or diaper change. This inspires little confidence in an era when we face the most horrifying virus of all time—the deadly AIDS epidemic. The World Health Organization estimates that by the year 2000 there will be ten million children infected with AIDS. The nightmare is magnified by the fact that most day-care institutions do not test for HIV positive children.

Let's face it, children in a group setting sometimes bite one another. They share toys that have been sucked or slobbered on by other children. Children going through toilet training have accidents. Parents should rightly be concerned about their children's exposure to such serious health problems easily received from other children.

In 1988 the city of New York established a frightening policy allowing toddlers and preschoolers with AIDS to attend day-care facilities throughout the city. About two hundred thousand non-infected children in two thousand public and private day-care centers were affected by the city order. The City Health Commissioner put teeth in the policy by threatening legal action against any day-care centers that tried to ignore it.[19] If this action serves as a precedent for other cities and municipalities, day-care centers may one day literally be crawling with HIV-infected toddlers and infants.

There are also *social ramifications* of day-care—for example, aggressive behavior. A comparative study by Ron Haskins of the University of North Carolina found that children placed in day-care during infancy are much more likely to hit, kick, push, threaten, swear, tease, and argue.[20] Since the Haskins research only corroborates earlier studies, it comes as little surprise.

Another social consideration of day-care is the continual "on" atmosphere which leaves children little time for noiseless contemplation and repose. An environment of large numbers of children continually talking and seeking stimulation and attention prods even quiet or reticent children to constantly react. Deborah Fallows, author of the book *A Mother's Work*, after spending hundreds of hours in dozens of centers in Massachusetts, Texas, Maryland, and Washington, D.C., noted an identity crisis in the depersonalized environment. Fallows observed that in her day-care visits she witnessed disturbing treatments of children (for example, being referred to as "hey, little girl") and activities that catered to the group but left quiet children behind. She speaks of desperate notes from parents begging that extra attention be given to their child.[21] It is impossible for such circumstances to not alter a child's personality.

There are other risks as well. Some parents cite cases of sexual abuse or physical battering. Many still remember the Virginia McMartin incident in California, in which a sweet-looking seventy-six-year-old woman and six of her coworkers were charged with molesting the little children trustingly placed under their care. Not long after this story made national headlines, similar ones began to surface. For example, in New York City it was divulged that managers of the Puerto Rican Association for Community Affairs Day-Care Center had raped, sodomized, and terrorized children.[22]

Recently my local newspaper carried a shocking story captioned, "Gonorrhea Found in 3 Toys at Florida Day-care Center." Rainbow

Learning Center, a Fort Lauderdale day-care center used by more than two hundred families, was the focal point of an investigation of gonorrhea transmission to three small children (ages two to four) in attendance there. Authorities identified thousands of nude photographs at the home of the center's owner, John Shaver.[23]

Such incidents have brought working parents to the stark realization that while they are earning extra income, their children are perhaps being subjected to fondling, sexual exploitation or rape. Often parents make a real effort to determine if a day-care provider is suitable, but later find they have been deceived.

This explains why the United States Congress has made millions of dollars available to the states for training child-care workers in order to prevent child abuse in licensed and regulated day-care facilities. Because of reported incidents of abuse, Congress continues to put pressure on the states to pass child abuse legislation.[24] But there are other problems inherent in the day-care industry that make protection against the myriad forms of child abuse difficult. For example, the industry suffers from a staff turnover rate of 40 percent and must get replacements quickly to meet state staff-child ratio requirements.[25] This makes it burdensome to do a nationwide criminal record check for prospective day-care attendants. Despite this, every state should mandate background checks for each potential employee of a public day-care facility. Unfortunately, even when this is done, states sometimes do not enforce their requirements. Most states have only one inspector for every seventy day-care centers, and some states inspect only a random 10 or 20 percent sample annually.[26]

Throwing money at this problem does not provide a suitable solution. The plain truth of the matter is, it is getting more difficult to find people who will do for money what few of us will do for any reason but love.

The growing evidence of psychological, medical, and social damage from long term day-care is prompting many renowned authorities and researchers to take a clear stand against it. Educational psychologist Burton White, author of *A Parent's Guide to the First Three Years* and former director of the Harvard Preschool Project, regards the growing use of day-care as "a disaster" for children. Yale psychologist Edward Zigler has confessed that he is now "less confident than many of [his] colleagues about the effects of infant care and less sanguine about it being the major policy option" for helping American families.[27] Burton White explains:

> After more than 30 years of research on how children develop well, I would not think of putting an infant or toddler of my own into any substitute-care program on a full-time basis, especially a center-based program. Unless you have a very good reason, I urge you not to delegate the primary child-rearing task to anyone else during your child's first three years of life. Babies form their first human attachment only once.[28]

Perhaps the best way to conclude our look at the effects of day-care is through the eyes of a child. In the countless hours of counseling I have done with families, I was especially touched by the words of a certain little girl. Here is the essence of her simple, sincere comments:

> My mom says she has to work. Every morning she takes me to day-care. Sometimes it makes me really sad. I just want to stay home. I asked Mommy to stay home with me, but she says it helps our family buy the things we want. I just want to see Mommy more. What can I say so she'll stay home?

Needless to say, these words brought a lump to my throat. What would you say to this teary-eyed four-and-a-half-year-old? Maybe it is time we realize that the child's-eye view of day-care has been right all along.

Guiding Principle:

Day-care should be avoided at all costs. Young mothers should not seek full-time employment outside the home if a simple and modest home life that meets the basic necessities of the family is feasible without it.

THREE

Assaults on the Family, Part II

We have been examining some of the very real threats to our families, and we will now look at a few more. May we not be intimidated by these enemies of our homes, but rather let us fight the good fight of faith with the courage only Christ gives.

MENACE OF THE ONE-EYED MONSTER

Much television programming has grown so crude and objectionable that the value of owning a TV set has lost most of its entertainment value. Tragically, between the ages of six and eighteen children sit in front of the television set fifteen to sixteen thousand hours, compared to thirteen thousand hours spent in school. According to a *Nielsen Report of Television*, children watch thirty to thirty-one hours of television weekly, more time than any other activity except sleeping.[1] Any argument about the learning deprivation of children who are without a TV set is highly overstated. However, a California study of a half-million public school students in the sixth through twelfth grades did find that the more TV children watch, the worse they do scholastically.[2]

Adults too are consumed by television viewing—and are negatively affected by it. Creativity and desperately needed family communication are being sold for the dubious privilege of becoming a couch potato. Constant exposure to hours of degenerate programming is twisting Christians' values and is desensitizing them to morally impure activity. And this is exacting a terrible cost on family interrelationships.

In America, television helps formulate the images that mold and shape our culture. Who decides the content of the shows that captivate America? Producers and writers. What kind of people are they? A revealing poll by the American Enterprise Institute for Public Policy Research in Washington answers that question. Speaking of television writers:

- 45 percent profess no religion at all.
- 7 percent attend a religious service once a month.
- 80 percent do not regard homosexual relations as wrong.
- 97 percent favor abortion on demand.
- 75 percent call themselves political liberals.
- Only 17 percent condemn adultery.[3]

Are these the kinds of people you want to heavily influence the way you and your children think? Doesn't your family deserve to be shielded from their deceptions and lies? Shouldn't we rather "take captive every thought to make it obedient to Christ" (2 Corinthians 10:5)? When all the defensiveness and ballyhoo about the merits of TV are laid to rest, we can objectively see there is very little there which is worthy of our time or attention.

Arguments about television's net worth for news, sports, nature and religious shows, etc. loose their potency in light of how difficult it is to strictly confine oneself to that kind of programming. The programs being aired indicate what most people want to watch. Even if you are determined to only watch reruns of "Little House on the Prairie" or Walt Disney specials, I believe there are still three overwhelming arguments against watching television.

First, you have no control over what is advertised or how. Children are exposed to many thousands of commercials each year. TV stations advertise a prime-time movie by highlighting the most tempting scenes. The liquor industry bombards viewers with enticing mini-dramas that glamorize alcohol consumption. Some adults flippantly try to dismiss the effect of advertisements—"I tune out the commercials." Really? Sponsors pay hundreds of millions of dollars to advertising firms that know how to produce results. It is hard to guard your heart and mind when advertisers use it for a garbage dump.

Second, TV ratings are determined by the number of people who view a particular program. The more who watch, the more revenue that program produces. Hence, in a sense TV viewers subsidize the program they watch and the network that produces it. The opposite is also true. By abstaining from viewing television, you are exercising the power of the purse, which the sponsors understand all too well.

Third, TV not only robs a family of interaction time, but often passes on values that are questionable or downright objectionable. The average American home watches six hours and forty-eight minutes of television each day. That's about fifty to seventy-five thousand hours of television in a lifetime.[4] In those hours the average family views approximately 9,230 sex acts or implied sex acts a year on TV. Eighty-one percent of that sexual activity is outside the commitment of marriage.[5] The average sixteen-year-old has watched eighteen thousand murders on television.[6] That's an incredible amount of violence, murders, sex and foul language. Christians know the heart can be no cleaner than what is stored in it. "Above all else, guard your heart, for it is the wellspring of life" (Proverbs 4:23).

The content on much TV today is so inconsistent with Biblical values, it amazes me that so many Christians ardently defend personal viewing. We live in a society of TV addicts, but as with any addiction, few are willing to own up to it. Some of the symptoms of a TV junkie include the following:

- Denial of the addiction. This is seen in statements such as, "I can turn it off any time I want to."
- An overwhelming compulsion to flip the TV on throughout the day.
- A "daily need" to relax by watching television.
- Frequently viewing for hours on end.
- The inability to go without TV viewing for a few weeks at a time without experiencing such withdrawal symptoms as boredom, complaining, inactivity, etc.
- A sense of remorse over an inability to control personal viewing.

Every Christian owes it to his family to seriously examine himself or herself in to see whether in fact he or she is addicted in this way. I received a letter from a father not long ago who after twelve years of TV addiction got rid of his TV set. Said the father,

> It wasn't an easy thing to do. But the whole family was obviously hooked on television. The TV set would run out of control for most of the evening hours. I knew something had to be done. Since we tossed the TV set, we have spent most of our time together just talking. We didn't realize what we were missing! We have begun to really get to know each other like never before. My marital relationship has never been stronger! Thanks for your loving advice at the seminar, and keep us in your prayers.

What a testimonial. The value of family closeness has been restored, and familial separation from the world has been reclaimed.

Guiding Principle:

As much as is humanly possible, Christian families will avoid television and other environments over which they have no control, especially those that display immoral activity or suggestions or are addictive in nature.

SOCIETY'S ATTACK ON MORAL PROPRIETY

Many of today's children (and adults) accept immorality as a way of life. Moral looseness has grafted itself into the very heart of our society. In some public high schools the most pejorative label you can pin on a boy or girl is to call them a virgin, for our culture considers premarital virginity obsolete or old-fashioned. Many Christians' sons and daughters have a knowledge of God's will, but the cultural mind-set continually applies pressure and temptation to Christians of all ages. Many a

Christian boy and girl with good intentions has ended up a pawn in the societal game of acceptable immorality, and many Christian adults have as well.

Constant societal bombardment with sex-saturated messages and imagery have been a major factor in bringing about the loss of moral standards. Add to this the corruption of a healthy view of physical intimacy inside the proper boundaries of marital union and you have a recipe for disaster: a country overwhelmed with fornication, sexual diseases, unwanted pregnancies, physical abuse, and molestation. The result of rampant fornication has been a half a million pregnancies each year out of wedlock, thirty million cases of incurable genital herpes, and explosive numbers of new cases each year of chlamydia, gonorrhea, pelvic inflammatory disease, sterility, and AIDS. This is a staggering price for our nation's immorality and culture-wide sexual addiction.

Immoral suggestions and temptations are continually being thrown in our faces, often when we least expect it—at grocery and convenience stores, on billboards, in magazine ads, etc.—often at children's eye level. Christians can protect themselves against blatant temptation much of the time, but we must be ever vigilant for the casual or even subliminal intrusion. Immoral suggestion vigorously invites Christian families to contaminate their minds and hearts.

The growth of cultural immorality has taken place gradually and subtly. If you have ever traveled in the mountains, you understand what I mean. As you look down from a mountain pass, you can frequently see a part of the highway below. But as you begin driving, you quickly start to wind and curve, you go up and you go down, and then you wind and curve some more. Before long you become disoriented and lose your perspective. You're not sure which way is north or south. In a short time, or perhaps after much time, you arrive at the portion of the road you saw from a higher altitude. You weren't always quite sure where you were going while on the way, but you knew when you arrived at the bottom.

Similarly, Satan leads Christians to accept immorality gradually, after many twists and turns meant to confuse us. Rarely will he bring a Christian down overnight. But slowly, with the passing of time and the gradual wearing down of our defenses, we become prone to change. You've probably heard before that the way to cook a frog is to put him in cold water and increase the heat slowly. The frog is unable to identify the gradual rise in temperature, and soon you have a culinary delight—cooked frog legs.

Gradual cultural change has indeed pulled the thinking of many Christians along with it. Fifty years ago a couple kissing affectionately in public would have seemed decadent. But as society has changed, moving further and further from godly moral standards, Christian families have unwittingly gravitated in the same direction. Not long ago I was talking with a Christian mother of three. She has a good, honest, hard-working husband and three beautiful teenage daughters. This family faithfully attends church every Sunday, and the children have been raised to love God and respect authority. As she wept and pushed away the tears she asked me, "Why did two of my daughters get involved with immorality? I just can't understand it. Our lifestyle hasn't been perfect, but it has been just as Christian as most other homes."

It is true that children can become wayward even after giving them the best upbringing possible. We know this from the Parable of the Prodigal Son in Luke 15. Yet, I think it is time we realize that having a home "just as Christian as the next" does not necessarily go far enough. Let's face it—many Christian homes have been polluted by the world. If there was ever an area where Christians need to get out of step with cultural mores, it is in those areas which tempt families towards moral impurity.

If there was ever a time to break ranks, now is the time. You can't change the whole world, but you can avoid exposure to some of its vices. It takes real leadership and spiritual courage to act in defense of your family's moral decency and purity. Some hope the problems won't affect their children. Others talk about how bad things are, but do little more than wink at the issues. *Uncompromising Christians don't just wish for a solution—they act.* We need more Christians with backbone—believers who will take the offensive, put greater moral safeguards in place, and speak out for Jesus Christ.

Moral leniency of necessity corrupts our souls and the souls of our children. Tolerance of impure activity desensitizes us and our children and makes us all vulnerable to the enemy's deceits. The crying need of the hour is not for self-imposed censorship, but rather for what the Bible calls *self-control*. ". . . the fruit of the Spirit is . . . self-control" (Galatians 5:22, 23). "Religion that God our Father accepts as pure and faultless is this: . . . to keep oneself from being polluted by the world" (James 1:27). There is only one way to keep our families from being spiritually polluted, and that is to control or limit its impact upon our daily lives through the power of the Holy Spirit. ". . . live by the Spirit, and you will not gratify the desires of the sinful nature" (Galatians 5:16).

Guiding Principle:
We must choose continually to avoid activities and environments where immorality is likely to be foisted upon us or our children.

MESMERIZED BY MATERIALISM

As we consider the impact of material prosperity on family life in America, we must ask in all sincerity, "Has it been a blessing or a curse?" When spirituality gives way to the desire for worldly possessions, family life is placed at the mercy of materialistic slavery. The more prosperous the nation, the greater the danger of possessiveness. Most Americans are considered rich by worldly standards. Unfortunately, many Christian families have stood in too much awe of material prosperity.

Prevalent cultural attitudes tell us to continually seek larger homes, salaries/bank accounts, newer automobiles, and the latest in VCRs/televisions, stereos, personal computers, kitchen appliances, and other electronic gadgetry. We are experiencing materialistic overkill. We have come to expect more and more modern conveniences with all the bells and whistles we think we deserve. The Christmas expectations of most American children (and adults, for that matter) are unjustifiable. No wonder! Prior to Christmas they are bombarded by clever store displays and catalogs (conveniently called "wish books") and mesmerized by alluring television commercials. Think of the dollars we have spent on some of our personal pleasures and comforts. What did these things accomplish? Honesty forces us to confess that the joy and value of material things last as long as a puff of smoke.

Too many of us engage in a relentless endeavor to search indefinitely for the full life materialism promises. Everyone is just on the verge; "maybe *this* will bring me satisfaction." We obtain the thing we wanted, but it doesn't bring happiness. So we think maybe something else will do the trick. And on and on the quest goes. It's time we stop our materialistic tailspin long enough to ask, "Where, if ever, does all this seeking and accumulating end?" Even if we owned a palatial home, luxury automobile, RV, and club membership, owned every last stock and bond, accumulated every piece of real estate both domestic and foreign, every last ounce of precious metal—indeed, all the wealth of the world—what would it profit? It would not move us any closer to fulfilling the purpose of our existence.

Materialism is a catch-22. We trade our time, our efforts, our skill, indeed our very lives, to obtain money. Then we spend a great deal of that money on many things that have little or no value. American garages, basements, and attics are full of useless, unfulfilling junk we have collected over the years. The popularity of garage sales tells us this is true. Worst of all, it is impossible to recover the time we squander on the purchase of worthless possessions. *Lord, free us from the tyranny of things!*

Much of the Christian community has unfortunately bought into this materialistic mind-set. Christian parents get caught in the game of chasing the so-called "almighty dollar," while their children pay the price of neglect and the neighborhood lacks a credible Christian witness. Too many Christians work hard to expand their influence and elevate their lifestyle while the world around them is dying in spiritual decay. Churches go into debt building expensive structures for affluent suburbanites, purchasing new red carpet and stained-glass windows, while at the same time missionaries are forced home for lack of funds. Yes, the American evangelical church spends money on evangelism. Yes, she supports such worthy causes as sending clothing, food and medicine to needy populations. But proportionally the American church spends more on herself than on propagating the gospel around the globe. (See the chart "Percent of Christian Money Spent on World Population" in Appendix D.)

It's time for serious Christians to come to the recognition of three spiritual facts in regard to this issue. First, *a proper reaction to cultural materialism confirms our salvation and reveals our spiritual maturity level.* It is imperative that we understand the proper place of material things in relation to the Lordship of Jesus Christ.

The second spiritual fact is this: *a right reaction to cultural materialism reflects our priorities.* If an investigator were to follow the money trail of our checkbook and credit-card purchases, what priorities would he see? Jesus drew a dividing line between worldly and spiritual priorities when He said, ". . . where your treasure is, there your heart will be also" (Matthew 6:21). Material indulgence and conspicuous consumption of worldly things run counter to the Christian message of seeking our treasure in Jesus Christ.

Third, *our reaction to cultural materialism will enhance or detract from our Christian witness.* We should each ask, "Am I different in my approach to and use of possessions than the culture I live in? If so, how? Does my lifestyle show that I put Jesus Christ ahead of all else?" When all is said and done, if we are not visibly different than the world around us, we are detracting from the effectiveness of our witness. The Achilles' heel of the Western Christian is, minimizing the importance of God and seeking comfort in money and material possessions.

Dietrich Bonhoeffer summarized this all quite well in saying, "The life of discipleship can only be maintained so long as nothing is allowed to come between Christ and ourselves."

Guiding Principle:

If we are not content with what we have, we will not be content by obtaining more of what we do not have. We must seek our riches in Jesus Christ!

We have seen in these first three chapters that the challenges to the family are indeed great. But they can be overcome by radical Christian living. In the pages that follow we will examine the Scriptural basis for such living.

FOUR

Families Following the Master

When Jesus walked this earth, He gave a clear command to His followers:

> "You are the salt of the earth. But if the salt loses its saltiness, how can it be made salty again? It is no longer good for anything, except to be thrown out and trampled by men. You are the light of the world. A city on a hill cannot be hidden. Neither do people light a lamp and put it under a bowl. Instead they put it on its stand, and and it gives light to everyone in the house. In the same way, let your light shine before men, that they may see your good deeds and praise your Father in heaven." (Matthew 5:13-16)

With these historic words our Lord drew an unmistakable line of demarcation between committed Christians and those who are compromising, accommodating and non-confrontational. He didn't say, "Think about being salty" or "Be salty if it makes people like you." He said, "You are the salt of the earth . . . You are the light of the world." If we are to be obedient to Him, we must act like it!

Today the heart-cry of Jesus to Christian men and women and to Christian families is the same. He wants us to be the salt and light of the world! *Jesus calls His people to be radical New Testament followers of Him.* Radical Christian families eagerly seek growth in spirituality, holiness, and evangelistic zeal. These priorities order Christian families' way of life and set them apart from the complacent and the spiritually lethargic.

We are not called to be spiritual hermits—sincere worshipers out of touch with those around us. Instead, we are called to make an impact on our world. We are asked to be salt to a tasteless and unsavory humanity, light within a society of darkness. All the while we are to maintain a delicate balance—in the world, but not of it.

The first way we know this is by looking at *our Lord's own life*. His birth was radical, His ministry and teaching were radical, His death and miraculous resurrection were radical. Everything about Him radiated enthusiasm and total commitment to the cause and purpose of Almighty God. Jesus wants His followers to imitate Him.

Jesus' radical nature not only made an impact on others—it subjected Him to tremendous criticism. The world's priorities ran completely opposite to the Lord Jesus Christ's. He could not have been chummy with the world and its pleasures and still accomplished His redeeming work. He could not have winked at sin and still have made a difference. His mission of reconciling the world to God required holiness, separation, and a radical way of life. We are called to do no less. The challenge of today's Christian families is to separate ourselves from sin and to be consecrated to Him. Christians' homes ought to be in sharp contrast to those of this world.

Because Jesus was judged by the world's standards, He was hated. And He forewarned His disciples (and us): "If the world hates you, keep in mind that it hated me first. If you belonged to the world, it would love you as its own. As it is, you do not belong to the world, but I have chosen you out of the world. That is why the world hates you" (John 15:18, 19). Being hated by the world is an unpleasant consequence, but Jesus puts His stamp of approval on the obedient, calling those hated for His name's sake "blessed" (Luke 6:22).

Radical Christianity can also bring conflict within one's own family. Jesus said:

"For I have come to turn 'a man against his father, a daughter against her mother, a daughter-in-law against her mother-in-law—a man's enemies will be the members of his own household.' Anyone who loves his father or mother more than me is not worthy of me; anyone who loves his son or daughter more than me is not worthy of me. . . ." (Matthew 10:35-37)

It is hard when a mother does not understand her daughter's way of life. It is trying when a father ridicules or ignores his son because of his beliefs or convictions. It is difficult when brother and sister are divided in their allegiance and priorities. But these are consequences followers of Christ must bear.

We love our parents and relatives dearly. However, if they are unsaved or are vacillating, non-committed Christians, their influence can weaken our commitment to Christ. To the man in Luke 9 Jesus said, "Follow Me." The man responded conditionally by saying, "I will follow you, Lord; but first let me go back and say good-by to my family." That sounds reasonable enough. But Jesus replied, "No one who puts his hand to the plow and looks back is fit for service in the kingdom of God" (Luke 9:61, 62). Jesus knew that unsaved friends and relatives can cause a man to stumble. *Whenever the heart starts looking back with longing to a former way of life, the believer is at that time not fit for Christian service.* The call of Jesus demands total commitment with no looking back.

Not all the consequences of radical commitment are negative. For example, Peter speaks about an "inexpressible and glorious joy" (1 Peter 1:8) that grips the lives of all who truly live for Jesus Christ. Radical Christians also have a rich measure of the nine-fold fruit of the Spirit: "love, joy, peace, patience, kindness, goodness, faithfulness, gentleness and self control" (Galatians 5:22, 23). Who can estimate the far-reaching effects of these fruits in our lives and in the lives of family members as we stay close to Jesus Christ?

A second way we know that Jesus calls us to a radical New Testament way of life is: *His hatred of spiritual mediocrity.* Jesus has said,

"I know your deeds, that you are neither cold nor hot." Then, regarding those who are *lukewarm*, He says, "I am about to spit you out of my mouth" (Revelation 3:15, 16). We know that Jesus would not spit true believers out of His Kingdom, but these words are an indictment against a halfhearted commitment. It's grievous that so many Christians today have mediocre standards and a Milquetoast lifestyle. Non-confrontational Christians are jellyfish who float along with prevailing cultural currents, doing little good for the cause of the Kingdom of God on earth.

CALLED TO BE SALT

Jesus compared Christians to salt. At the time of Jesus salt served at least five purposes: 1) As a condiment. This function is self-evident since we continue to use salt to make our food more palatable. Long ago Job asked, "Is tasteless food eaten without salt?" (Job 6:6). 2) As a preservative. 3) As a ceremonial ingredient on sacrifices. 4) For medicinal purposes. And 5) for economic purposes. In the early New Testament world, salt, being so scarce and precious, was used as money. In fact, Roman soldiers received part of their pay in common salt. This government dole was known as their *salarium*, from which we get the word *salary*. In some areas salt was said to have been traded ounce for ounce for gold. In ancient Greece it was even common to exchange salt for slaves, which gave us the phrase "not worth his salt." [1]

Of all salt's purposes, its *purifying and preserving* nature was the most treasured. Since the introduction of refrigeration, salt has lost this basic purpose in most homes. When Jesus told His followers they were to be the salt of the earth, He was declaring them to be moral and spiritual preservers in the world. We are to be a preserving power, an antiseptic, an agent to prevent and retard decay. The most effective preservers are those who are involved, conscientious, concerned citizens, followers of Christ who know what it means to be righteous and responsible. Many major legislative victories favoring moral purity have been won by a handful of radical Christians.

NOT CALLED TO A LIFESTYLE OF STEALTH

Christians are also called upon to be *light* in a dark world, the bearers of the Good News of salvation through Jesus Christ. A Christian cannot carry out his true calling if he does not let it be known that he is a Christian. Jesus said, "... let your light shine before men, that they may see your good deeds and praise your Father in heaven" (Matthew 5:16). Though darkness continually seeks to extinguish it, the light generated from a radical New Testament Christian cannot be snuffed out!

In a sin-filled world ruled by the prince of darkness, the nature of light is quite clear—it exposes sin and reveals truth! The children's chorus says it well: "This little light of mine, I'm going to let it shine." On the darkest night a small candle can be seen burning for over a mile. Light overpowers darkness! One zealous, on-fire Christian can lead hundreds, even thousands of people to the Lord in his lifetime. Our lives should be such that those around us clearly know the way to Heaven, even if they know little else about us.

We must recognize that at times our light will attract and at times it will repel, for so it was with the light of Jesus. "To the one we are the smell of death; to the other, the fragrance of life" (2 Corinthians 2:16). Radical Christians diffuse everywhere the presence of Christ, which has different effects on believers and unbelievers. But one thing is sure—our light must shine on!

Unfortunately, the Christian community has often lost its saltiness and has hidden its light under a basket. We cannot truly be salt and light without learning how to guard ourselves from spiritual compromise. And as we walk and grow in holiness, we will not only more truly be salt and light, but our family life will flourish as well. Radical, committed Christianity is the best way to ensure our family's optimal health in the secular, humanistic culture in which we live. Under our Lord's guidance, as we faithfully follow Him, we can build a strong family and fulfill our life's mission in the process.

Living as a flourishing Christian family in a world committed to its own selfish lusts is admittedly difficult. But the prognosis is good for those willing to take a radical Christian stand.

Guiding Principle:
The Christian family will make its calling to be salt and light to others a top priority and a concern of urgent prayer.

FIVE
Faithful in a Fallen Culture

The religious value structure of the United States has been systematically eroding for decades. As a result, Christian values become more and more minimized or even hated within our culture. The secular paganism in our society is stronger than ever. We Christians must learn how to have a purifying influence on the society in which we live.

Radical Christian families must find a healthy middle ground between isolation and cultural entanglement. The American lifestyle has many spiritual and social ailments, all of which can be contagious. How can we be faithful to the Christian call while limiting our families' exposure to spiritual malignancies? How can we have a greater influence on our culture than our culture has on us?

INTERACTING WITH OUR CULTURE

Truth #1:
Hiding Is Not an Option

The Roman Empire, which controlled the world from 30 B.C. to the fifth century A.D., was the precursor of modern Western society. The Roman governmental structure dominated and unified a confederation of city-states. The Empire had a massive highway system, a common currency, and a powerful military which conspicuously imposed its absolute will around the Mediterranean world and western Europe. During the first century of the Christian era, there were on active duty approximately twenty-eight well-armed legions, with a maximum of six thousand officers and men per legion.[1] Taxes levied on the civilian population almost continually increased. As the Empire grew, it struggled with common domestic problems such as unemployment, inadequate housing, and urban sprawl. Sounds familiar, doesn't it?

At the peak of the Empire, material wealth was commonplace among the cosmopolitan population. Theater, sports, and other forms of public entertainment became predominant national pastimes. There were three dominant theaters in Paul's day: one in Pompeii which seated ten thousand, another in Balbus which seated eight thousand, and a third in Marcellus that seated fourteen thousand. Roman life also offered gymnasiums, public baths, and sea cruises.[2]

Modern American society reflects a preoccupation with many of the same values the Romans held dear. Instead of open theaters we have huge, domed sports stadiums; in place of bathhouses we have public hot tubs and swimming pools. Like the Romans, our society engages in an endless quest for pleasure, social gaiety, and sexual gratification outside the boundaries of marriage.

The Roman Empire is an ancient prototype of America spiritually as well. In the Roman Empire secularism and state-supported paganism flourished. Magnificent temples and monuments were erected to venerate the gods and goddesses of man-created, Greco-Roman mythology. After A.D. 180, the floodgates of syncretism opened, ushering in superstition, magic, astrology, mystery cults, and occultism.

Like the Roman culture of old, America is being engulfed by vacuous religiosity, paganism, and outright occultic activity. Judicial activism that throws the Bible (1963: *Schempp v. Murray*) and voluntary prayer (1971: *Netcong*) out of public schoolrooms and that legalizes abortion (1973: *Roe v. Wade*) are prime examples of governmental participation in the heathenizing of our culture. Like Rome, we are witnessing state-sponsored paganism.

Though we may not like to admit it, America is not very different from the ancient world. Corinth was decadent and immoral, and so is

American culture. Gladiatorial Rome had a strong lust for pleasure and sports, and so do we. The philosophical geniuses of Athens prided themselves on their intellectual superiority and ingenuity, and so does twentieth-century man. Idolatrous Ephesus had many superstitions and cultic activities, and so do we. The Roman Empire had to contend with the hollow shell of religious customs and ritual, and we are plagued with much religiosity and dead, powerless churches. Furthermore, we are every bit as materialistic as the fallen Empire of old—even more so.

The challenges Christian families face in America are not new; they were faced centuries ago. Considering the cultural parallels between Rome and America, we can learn a great deal from the lifestyle and response of the early Christians. Life was very difficult in those days, for they battled cultural immorality, materialism, humanism, and blatant idolatry. But they stood their ground! Ultimately a choice between emperor worship or civil disobedience was thrust upon them, and obedience to Christ often meant martyrdom.

The early Christians did not arbitrarily break off all contact with those who rejected God's sovereignty or the gospel message, nor did they isolate themselves from the heathen they were called to reach. Jesus Himself did not live in seclusion from the evils of the Roman Empire. He spent time with "sinners" and tax collectors—people like Zacchaeus, the rich young ruler, and the harlot who washed His feet with her tears. On one occasion He said, "It is not the healthy who need a doctor, but the sick. I have not come to call the righteous, but sinners" (Mark 2:17).

When the Apostle Paul walked into Athens and saw that city full of idols, he didn't shout out, "You blasphemous, wretched pagan idolaters! You deserve God's judgment!" Instead, he was "greatly distressed" by what he saw, and he used what he learned from their environment to build his evangelistic message (Acts 17:16ff.). When he wrote his first letter to the Corinthian believers, he didn't tell them to withdraw themselves from the decadence of their society, for to do that they would "have to leave this world." To the contrary, he admonished them to be more concerned about the decadence within their own churches (1 Corinthians 5:9-11).

Hiding from an evil environment does not help solve the spiritual dilemma of mankind. Rather, Christian families are called on to provide Biblical answers. Salvation is freely offered to all people in Jesus Christ. It's our job to proclaim that message in a credible and intelligent way.

As we have previously mentioned, radical Christianity touches culture in two ways—as salt and as light. To be light in this world means we must go into the darkness, winning as many people as we can to Jesus Christ. Ignoring or running away from societal problems is a cowardly and faithless approach, leaving Christians without purpose and the world without hope. The Good News of the Lord Jesus Christ is the only answer for the world's desperate needs.

We cannot change our culture by living in spiritual seclusion. Rather, as committed Christians we are to work unceasingly to make Christ's message known and to influence the present world for good. We must both acknowledge the problems of our society and work to resolve them.

Guiding Principle:

As far as is possible and reasonable, Christian families must insulate themselves from ungodly cultural influence and activity without isolating themselves. Christians are called to witness and to warfare!

Contact with the world is necessary if we are to maintain a credible witness. But without insulation from the world's evils Christians will only produce a small amount of life- or world-changing fruit. If we walk wisely, there is no limit to what Christ can do through us. Our job is to run the race set before us and to do all we can to bring Him glory.

As long as we are on the earth, we must work untiringly to help people and governments renounce their independence and submit to the Lordship of Jesus Christ. We must labor zealously to establish righteousness and positive change. The secularist believes that to change man you must change his culture, while the Christian believes that to change culture you must change man. This cannot accomplished by Christians in hiding.

Truth #2: Christian Activism Is Essential in a Corrupt Culture

Some well-intentioned Christians insist that God's people are to concentrate solely on spiritual matters. But Scripture is replete with examples of God using committed men and women to represent Him in the political arena. Joseph used his political opportunities to influence Pharaoh. Hilkiah and Shaphan used their positions to influence Josiah. Daniel was deeply involved in governmental affairs. In fact, he was one of the top rulers under the reign of three kings—Nebuchadnezzar, Belshazzar, and Darius. Daniel so influenced King Darius that the king decreed, "[I]n every part of my kingdom people must fear and reverence the God of Daniel" (Daniel 6:26). Esther and Nehemiah both used their positions to influence public policy. John the Baptist boldly spoke against corruption in the political and ecclesiastical structures of his day, and ultimately lost his life because of his stand.

Christians are commanded to "occupy" until Jesus comes (Luke 19:13, KJV) and to "hate evil" (Proverbs 8:13). To condemn evil with our lips but allow it to flourish by our inaction is inconsistent with Biblical injunction. Edmund Burke has rightly stated, "All that is necessary for the triumph of evil is for good men to do nothing." Hoping and wishing for righteousness to take root will not make it a reality. It is the privilege—and responsibility—of Christian families in America to use their influence, however great or small, to ensure that righteousness rules in government and in all levels of society. Prayer is extremely important, but so is personal intervention and involvement.

We need more Christians who walk wisely in the power of the

Holy Spirit—who are "as shrewd as serpents and as innocent as doves" (Matthew 10:16). We need well-read men and women who stay informed and who can speak rationally and responsibly to our culture about the necessity of righteousness, moral integrity, and a pro-family ethos. It's not enough for Christians to shout "Amen" as we spout jargon already acceptable amongst ourselves. We must appeal to the mainstream of society using intelligent, Biblical arguments. We must be able to aptly say, "God's Word says . . ." Further, it is imperative that we teach our children about these matters—and that we model the Christian response so our children can see for themselves how these things work in practical life.

If we are going to successfully influence our culture, it is imperative that we appeal to reason and good sense. The media tend to characterize Christians as backwoods, Bible-thumping bigots. Unfortunately, certain elements in the Christian community contribute to that reputation by continually pontificating trite slogans and hackneyed religious clichés. Such approaches do not move our culture towards the desired end of greater righteousness.

If we are going to have an impact on our world, we must learn how to articulate our views in an effective and intelligent manner.[3]

Ecclesiastical Narcolepsy?

Christians are called to be the conscience of their nation. To do this they must be alert and informed and take a vigorous lead in fighting for righteousness and social change. If across our ranks Christians were as politically active in fighting pornography as the political liberals have been in promoting it, how different the situation would be! *If American freedoms are to survive, Christian activism must become the hallmark of the nineties.* Perhaps the first step in doing this is to discuss the issues in our homes and pray about them fervently. Family prayer is a great weapon for God!

God has not left us without rules and guidelines for government. He commands that there be righteous rulers and a system of government based on moral law. His Word clearly states that "Righteousness exalts a nation, but sin is a disgrace to any people" (Proverbs 14:34). Accountability is necessary if government is going to fulfill its ordained role of protecting the innocent from the wicked. When government refuses to do this, political repression follows (Proverbs 28:15), and political repression always brings religious repression. This is serious business, for when sin is allowed to reign in government, God's judgment comes upon the whole nation. (For an example of this, see 2 Chronicles 28:19.) Do we truly believe this? Have we transmitted these truths to our sons and daughters?

Christians must both take an active role in the governmental process and hold government answerable for its actions. Some erroneously teach that all individual rulers (instead of governmental authority in general) are ordained by God. However, Hosea 8:4 clearly indicates that a nation can select unrighteous rulers in violation of God's will. Thus, many Christians have mistakenly come to believe that political involvement is not the responsibility of the church. However, historically Christianity has often been in the forefront of reforming societal injustices. For example, it was Christianity that initially elevated the status of women. (Pagan cultures in foreign lands still treat women with great degradation.) Christians were also instrumental in bringing victory to the anti-slavery movement. And it was Christians who helped stop a Hindu custom in India in which widows threw themselves on funeral biers.

Common Excuses for Personal Political Non-involvement

One way Christians justify their inaction is with the excuse, "The problem is so big, and evil is so entrenched, there is really not much I can do." We are not called to solve every evil that plagues the world. But if every Christian would be willing to fight the good fight of faith in just one or two areas, the world would become a much better place to live and God would be glorified.

Some justify lack of personal involvement by phrasing the same excuse a little differently: "I'm only one person. What can one person do?" Everett Hale once said:

I am only one,
but I am one.
I cannot do everything,
but I can do something.
What I can do, I should do
and, with the help of God, I will do!

Anything you do to promote righteousness is Christ-honoring. For example, you can cast only one vote in an election, but remember:

- One vote gave America the English language instead of German.
- Thomas Jefferson and John Quincy Adams were elected President by one vote in the Electoral College. . . .
- One vote changed France from a monarchy to a republic.
- One vote gave Adolf Hitler leadership of the Nazi party.
- One vote per precinct elected John Kennedy President of the United States.[4]

Families flourish when righteous men govern, and they cease to flourish when unjust men rule. "When the righteous are in authority, the people rejoice; but when the wicked beareth rule, the people mourn" (Proverbs 29:2, KJV). Societal contempt for Christianity goes hand in hand with contempt for morality and the family. That is why Christians must be active in many areas of public responsibility.

It's important that you write your elected representatives often. Communicate your views on bills currently before Congress that could negatively affect traditional values, family life, and religious freedom. At election time be sure to cast your ballot for good candidates. Encourage competent Christians to run for office—and be open to running yourself. Help your pastor and church board become informed about critical issues. Financially support good candidates as much as possible. Get involved in one or two issues that are important to Christianity, righteousness, freedom, and the family.

Here are twenty specific ways we can all become personally involved:

1) Financially support organizations defending democracy, morality and religious freedom, including:

Rutherford Institute
P.O. Box 7482
Charlottesville, VA 22906-7482
(804) 978-3888

Eagle Forum
P. O. Box 618
Alton, IL 62002
(618) 462-5415

Concerned Women for America
370 L'Enfant Promenade S.W.
Suite 800
Washington, DC 20024
(202) 488-7000

National Legal Foundation
P.O. Box 64845
Virginia Beach, VA 23464
(804) 424-4242

Christian Legal Society
P.O. Box 1492
Merrifield, VA 22116-1492
(703) 642-1070

President's Council
P.O. Box 40
Fort Lauderdale, FL 33302-0040
(305) 771-8840

American Family Association
P.O. Box 2440
Tupelo, MS 38803
(601) 844-5036

2) Form a community action league to fight pornography; or if one already exists, join it. The National Coalition Against Pornography can help you start your own local organization and will gladly assist you in staging a citywide campaign against obscenity.

NCAP
800 Compton Road
Suite 9224
Cincinnati, OH 45231

3) Visit or write your local district attorney and ask if the obscenity statutes are being enforced in your city or county. Also, regularly write letters to the editor of your local newspaper in support of issues that affect family life.

4) Encourage your church to show the anti-pornography video *A Winnable War*, or the pro-life videos *The Silent Scream* and *Operation Rescue*.

5) Support local crisis pregnancy centers financially and by volunteering your time and talents. Encourage your church to commemorate Human Life Sunday annually.

6) Open your home to a needy pregnant woman until she can bear her child.

7) Lovingly picket an abortion clinic and attempt to persuade young women to let their babies live.

8) Raise money to donate pro-family books to your local library.

9) Run for your local library board.

10) Take advantage of opportunities in your local public school district to review textbooks being considered. Let the school board know of any anti-religious or immoral biases in the books. Consider running for the school board yourself.

11) Acquaint your local school board with quality sex education curricula that emphasize abstinence.

12) Find out if your local phone company has dropped its dial-a-porn service; if not, start a campaign against it.

13) Start a social action committee at your church. Teach a Sunday school class on social action issues in which Christians can get involved.

14) Help promote moral decency and human rights by fighting the advance of militant homosexual propaganda in classrooms and legislatures.

15) Monitor local judges and their decisions, keeping in mind that many of these jurists face re-election contests. Hold them accountable. Publicize a list of state and local judges who are pro-family and who are anti-family. Encourage Christian lawyers to run for judgeships.

16) Join a hospital ethics committee, or monitor the decisions of the existing committee.

17) Speak on moral/social issues at your local PTA, Rotary, Lions, or Kiwanis meetings.

18) Join your political party's local precinct committee and work to promote a moral platform.

19) Teach a chastity class in your church to teens and preteens. Encourage your pastor to take a clear, loving stand on moral issues.

20) Join a local pro-life group, or a state coalition. For more information contact:

Right To Life
419 7th Street N.W.
Suite 500
Washington DC 20004
(202) 626-8800

Reap Resources
Box 2035
Binghamton, NY 13902
(607) 772-6750[5]

There are many legal ways Christians can take a public stand in defense of righteousness. For example, I believe every Christian should actively support the pro-life movement. This is something Christian families can do together. We can promote the sanctity of human life by participating in pro-life rallies or non-violent protest marches, picketing clinics, or promoting boycotts of hospitals and physicians that participate in abortive procedures. One form of picketing is called "life chains." Thousands of Christians stand six to eight feet apart along a predetermined route for an hour or two after church on Sunday. The goal is to hold signs with bold letters that say such things as, ABORTION IS MURDER! For information about getting a life chain started in your area contact:

Please Let Me Live
3209 Colusa Highway
Yuba City, CA 95993
(916) 671-5500

Other ways our families can help the pro-life cause include untiring prayer, generous financial contributions, and the dissemination of timely information.

A second way Christians opt out of personal involvement is by saying, "Separation of church and state prohibits me from influencing public policy." Interestingly enough, the oft-quoted phrase "wall of separation" is nowhere found in the Constitution, and neither is "church and state." The origin of the phrase "wall of separation between church and state" actually comes from a letter written by Thomas Jefferson in 1802.[6] Since that time, his statement has been grossly misinterpreted and misapplied to mean separation of God and His people from government.

Secular humanists, often operating within the confines of the church, have convinced many Christians it is wrong to be active in politics. However, the committed Christian understands that in a democratic society he ought to use his constitutional rights to further the growth and expansion of godliness. If more Christians would have spoken out fifty years beforehand, Hitler may never have risen to power. Many Christians even kept silent as six million Jews were being slaughtered.

A third way believers excuse their inactivity is by stating, "Jesus and the disciples never tried to change the Roman government." *Changing government is not our goal.* Rather, our goal is to be responsible citizens in keeping with Christ's command to be the salt (the moral purifier) of the earth.

We who live in a democratic republic have a unique opportunity, for our freedom encourages participation. For a Christian to shirk his democratic duty—i.e., active and vocal involvement—is to disobey God and His Word.[7] Daniel Webster once said, "Whatever makes men good Christians makes them good citizens." What a witness this can be!

Christians are indeed to submit to established authority, in keeping with Romans 13. It is the government's job to bear the sword against wrongdoers and to punish them, and we need to teach our children to submit to political authority. But it is also our job as citizens to see that government wields the sword justly. The church of Jesus Christ must hold government morally accountable. Individually and as families we can carry out this task only if we are willing to pay the price of personal commitment and involvement.

Fourth, some excuse their inactivity with the words, "My faith is between me and God, and I refuse to push it onto other people." We certainly don't want to shove Christianity down anyone else's throat. At the same time, we dare not disregard our moral and civic responsibilities. Time and again, for example, we have heard political figures say they personally believe abortion is wrong, but they would never seek to impose their views on others. Christians who adopt this politically popular attitude are really saying, "My beliefs are personal. They don't have anything to do with anybody else." Such an attitude denies the Lordship of Jesus Christ and our personal responsibility as His disciples.

Some also offer the erroneous rhetoric, "You can't legislate morality." Actually, morality is being imposed on each of us every day. If we truly believe morality can't be legislated, why don't we take down all the speed limit signs, eliminate all traffic lights, and close down all police departments? Because they *work*. Every law imposes some sort of moral standard on society, and rightly so.

Guiding Principle:

As God's people on earth, we must face the awful realities of our fallen society, choose to go beyond our excuses for non-involvement, and bravely lead the way in knowing and serving the God of Heaven.

Truth #3: Interacting with Culture Can Be Difficult and Lonely

"Help! My relatives are not Christians. If I spend too much time with them, their worldly attitudes will pull me down. What should I do?" Families, both nuclear and extended, are sometimes separated by one's faith in Jesus Christ. Jesus said, "If anyone comes to me and does not hate his father and mother, his wife and children, his brothers and sisters—yes, even his own life—he cannot be my disciple" (Luke 14:25). Jesus is saying, "You cannot be My disciple if you love your father, mother, wife or children *more than you love Me*."

Our Lord was even more specific in Matthew: "Do not suppose that I have come to bring peace to the earth. I did not come to bring peace, but a sword. For I have come to turn 'a man against his father, a daughter against her mother, a daughter-in-law against her mother-in-law—a man's enemies will be the members of his own household'" (10:34). Intra-family conflict is inevitable unless all members are living for Jesus.

Such separation also occurs between carnal and committed Christians. Radical Christians avoid intense or prolonged socialization with anyone who will cause them to jeopardize their commitment to Christ. This may mean purposely distancing ourselves from friends and relatives who have a compromised Christian walk. Such a stand may result in criticism and rejection, but obedience to the Master must always take priority.

This does not preclude worshiping with those whose lifestyle is inconsistent with their confession, or studying God's Word with them, or discipling and assisting them. However, the situation does make it impossible to be among their closest friends. A reasonable degree of distancing should take place when you see more harm than good coming out of the relationship.

Also, mature Christians are the spiritual leaders of this world, and leadership is often lonely. As Moses led his people toward the Promised Land, he was continually harassed by their criticisms of his leadership and by their worldliness and idolatry. On one occasion in utter frustration Moses poured out to God the burden of his loneliness:

> "What have I done to displease you that you put the burden of all these people on me? Did I conceive all these people? Did I give them birth? Why do you tell me to carry them in my arms, as a nurse carries an infant, to the land you promised on oath to their forefathers? . . . If this is how you are going to treat me, put me to death right now—if I have found favor in your eyes—and do not let me face my own ruin." (Numbers 11:11, 12, 15)

Spiritual leadership can be very lonely. One wonders how our Lord—the greatest leader of all—must have felt as He walked in a world filled with spiritual rebellion. He certainly felt it important to at times be alone in order to renew His strength. Hence a walk of holiness is of necessity a walk of measured separation and, occasionally, loneliness.

Guiding Principle:
Despite the difficulties and loneliness of radical Christianity, we must choose again and again to be faithful to the One who has called us to follow Him.

Truth #4: Living Righteously Brings Blessing and Persecution

While we lose some relationships by being committed to Christ, we also gain new ones. Jesus said, "Truly I say to you, there is no one who has left house or brothers or sisters or mother or father or children or farms, for My sake and for the gospel's sake, but that *he shall receive a hundred times as much now in the present age*, houses and brothers and sisters and mothers and children and farms, *along with persecutions*; and in the world to come, eternal life" (Mark 10:29, 30, NASB). Jesus promises the reconstruction of all human relationships and affections spiritually as we sacrifice them on the altar because we love Him. Divine blessings replace worldly anxiety with thankfulness and imperishable treasures.

Jesus also mentioned persecutions as a part of the Christian experience in this life. But even they are a blessing, for by them we become stronger in the Lord. The unregenerate world hates what (or actually who) Christians stand for—Jesus Christ. Jesus said, "If they persecuted me, they will persecute you also" (John 15:20). Yet, "If you are insulted because of the name of Christ, you are blessed, for the Spirit of glory and of God rests on you" (1 Peter 4:14). As we encourage each other and our children to remain true to the Lord, we must in honest love tell them there will be a price, but that the Lord will be more to them than they will ever lose.

Wholesale persecution of Christians has not occurred in America to date, though I believe American Christianity is now under a form of persecution. Christianity has been tossed out of the public schools, and the Religious Right is openly ridiculed. Militant, unrepentant homosexuals have not only gained powerful political positions, but have also wormed their way into the church. For example, when one church discovered its youth director was homosexual, it politely asked for his resignation. Shortly thereafter it found itself in the middle of a lawsuit.

Given the mood of the legislatures and the tenure of our judicial system, churches and Christian ministries can expect to be increasingly challenged in court. It has been brought to my attention that the American Bar Association recently briefed its membership on the "gold mine" to be made in litigation against the Christian community.

We know that Christians who take a stand for righteousness will be persecuted in many ways, for "everyone who wants to live a godly life in Christ Jesus will be persecuted" (2 Timothy 3:12). Yet, as God's people we must speak out—we must take a stand for Christ, individually and as families.

Humanists smile as long as Christians are uninvolved, but the minute we start spreading salt outside the church, the humanists become enraged. Such worldly wrath is often followed by persecution, which merely indicates the believer is doing what he or she should be doing. Some Christians do all they can to avoid conflict. But radical Christians understand that suffering is the fruit of exclusive allegiance to Jesus Christ and the cause of righteousness. If we are under enemy attack, we can take heart, for persecution puts us in the company of the prophets, and we will share their high rewards (Matthew 5:10-12).

Guiding Principle:
Rather than always choosing the road of ease and comfort, radical Christians keep following Christ, no matter what the cost!

Truth #5: Committed Christians Are Always Few in Number

As Jesus Himself said, "But small is the gate and narrow the road that leads to life, and only a few find it" (Matthew 7:14). And of those calling themselves believers, only a small percentage are radically committed to the cause of Christ—a remnant of the remnant.

We should not be discouraged by the small number of committed Christians engaged in the battle, for it doesn't take many Christians to bring about great change. The vocal minority always accomplishes more than the silent majority. One genuine, fully committed believer plus

God is a majority. Consider the effectiveness of the small group of believers who penetrated the very heart of Antioch, the third-largest city in the Roman Empire with a population of half a million, where believers in Jesus were first dubbed *Christians*. Similarly, today many of the greatest legislative victories are achieved through a handful of Christian activists. Thus, neither we nor our children should turn aside because we feel outnumbered, or because of peer pressure; rather, we ought to be strong in the Lord and do His bidding with courage and delight. This is especially a key point for our teenage sons and daughters.

If others are halfhearted or indifferent to the fight, we should be all the more active and determined and not allow their coldness to harm the Master's cause. We must do everything in our power to get fellow Christians stirred up for the battle, but must not allow ourselves to become discouraged due to others' inaction. Do they compromise their convictions? May we be all the more resolute in our own! Are they critical, cynical, negative? Let us seek a greater fullness of love and faith!

Guiding Principle:

True Christians serve Christ, not the crowd! Allegiance to the Master must be protected and renewed however and whenever necessary.

WHY CIVIL DISOBEDIENCE IS SOMETIMES NECESSARY

While this subject is one of the hot-potato issues in the modern evangelical community today, it must be considered—especially since our government continues to sanction the slaying of innocent human life in abortion-on-demand.

If a Law of God is diametrically opposed to a human law, what are we and our families to do? *"We must obey God rather than men"* (Acts

5:29). Numerous Biblical examples demonstrate this crucial principle. Hebrew midwives lied rather than kill their babies (Exodus 1:15-21). (Lying is always wrong, but these women's fear of God and their courage in saving human lives were commended by God.) Moses was hidden in the reeds in violation of Pharaoh's edict (Exodus 1:22—2:10). Shadrach, Meshach and Abednego refused to worship the image of Nebuchadnezzar (Daniel 3:13-18). The Magi headed east from Bethlehem despite King Herod's orders (Matthew 2:7-12). Jesus healed a blind man (John 9:13-16) and a man with a withered hand (Luke 6:6-11) on the Sabbath. When Peter and John were told to stop preaching, they refused to obey (Acts 4:19, 20).

Through the centuries many courageous Christians have violated man-made laws in order to preserve lives or follow a higher moral law. We can cite such men and women of faith as Corrie ten Boom and André Trocmé, who both hid Jews during World War II—or Lee Coffin, who was the leader of the Underground Railroad in defiance of the Fugitive Slave Law. We ought to praise such believers, not condemn them. We and our children need to be crystal-clear on these matters, so we can give first priority to God and do whatever He asks of us.

Those who oppose civil disobedience remind us that Romans 13:1-7 instructs us to be subject to the governing authorities. Yes, that passage does in fact teach that! But the civil obedience commanded there is based on a government's providing just laws and rules. Either short of that or beyond that, Christians are not to obey! For example, abortion, which is murder, is a cardinal violation of one of God's commandments. The clear thrust of Scripture is that Christians are to obey the governing authorities in all matters which do not promote flagrant violation of God's moral laws. Abortion is without question a gross moral evil that must not be tolerated.

When is civil disobedience legitimate? Charles Colson, formerly special counsel to President Richard Nixon, properly identifies three occasions when civil disobedience can justifiably be carried out:

Civil disobedience is clearly justified when government attempts to take over the role of the church or allegiance due only to God. Then the Christian has not just the right but the duty to resist. The Bible gives a dramatic example of this in its account of three young Jewish exiles who were drafted into the Babylonian civil service. All citizens of Babylon were required to worship the statue of Nebuchadnezzar, the king; those who disobeyed were incinerated. Like many political leaders, power and authority were not enough for King Nebuchadnezzar; he wanted spiritual submission as well. Shadrach, Meshach, and Abednego, the young Hebrews, refused. To worship an earthly king would be the ultimate offense against their holy God. (Remember that the early Christians, in civil disobedience, refused to engage in Emperor worship and paid for it with their lives.)

... Civil disobedience is also mandated when the state restricts freedom of conscience, as in the case of Peter and John, two of Jesus' disciples. Peter and John were arrested for disturbing the peace. They were taken before the Sanhedrin, a religious body holding authority from the government of Rome, and ordered to stop preaching about Jesus. Peter and John refused. "Judge for yourselves whether it is right in God's sight to obey you rather than God," they said. "We cannot help speaking about what we have seen and heard." Their first allegiance was to the commandment they had been given by the resurrected Christ: the Great Commission to preach the gospel first to Jerusalem, then to the rest of Judea, and then to the ends of the earth. They could not permit the authority of the government-backed Sanhedrin to usurp the authority of God Himself.

... The third justification for civil disobedience is probably the most difficult to call. It is applied when the state flagrantly ignores its divinely mandated responsibilities to preserve life and maintain order and justice. Those last words are key for Christians in deciding to disobey civil authority. Civil disobedience is never undertaken lightly or merely to create disorder. Replacing one bad situation with another is no solution, but when the state becomes an instrument of the very thing God ordained it to restrain, the Christian must resist.[8]

Mr. Colson summarizes his view on civil disobedience in these words:

> Rightly exercised, civil disobedience is divine obedience. But when Christians engage in such activities, it must always be to demonstrate their submissiveness to God, not their defiance of government.
> ... Good citizenship requires both discernment and courage—discernment to soberly assess the issues and to know when duty calls one to obey or disobey, and courage, in the case of the latter, to take a stand.[9]

For over a decade and a half American courts have been sanctioning the abortion holocaust. Abortion did not become the law of the land by a majority vote of elected members of Congress, but through unelected judges practicing raw judicial activism. We Christians have voiced our protest to this moral outrage to little avail. We have prayed, voted, written our congressional representatives, and sought redress in the courts. While Christians rightly continue in those worthwhile activities, there was also a need for a more direct approach, and thus Operation Rescue was born. Operation Rescue is a coalition of pro-life Christian activists whose blockage of abortion clinics is coupled with passive resistance to police arrest. Their objective is not to *break the law*, but to *rescue helpless unborn children*. The Biblical mandate for engaging in such rescue operations includes Proverbs 24:11, 12—"Rescue those being led away to death; hold back those staggering toward slaughter. If you say, 'But we knew nothing about this,' does not he who weighs the heart perceive it? Does not he who guards your life know it? Will he not repay each person according to what he has done?" Abortion is a family issue, and each of our families must fight against it however God leads.

Obviously, before a Christian resorts to civil disobedience all reasonable alternatives must be exhausted. But there sometimes comes a point when normal channels (negotiation, legislation, judicial redress) fail to bring about a solution, and further action must then be taken. Constitutional attorney John Whitehead concurs: "Resistance and civil disobedience are legitimate reactions to tyrannous acts of the state."[10] Naturally we must guard against letting civil disobedience spill over into unmitigated violence. Neither should we get sidetracked on minor battles. Whitehead identifies priority concerns:

> The key priority issues certainly include: the sanctity of life; the protection of the traditional family; the church and the private school; and the freedom of the public arena (including public schools). This is not a checklist but a list of priorities which must be conscientiously dealt with simultaneously.[11]

Some in the church like to criticize the efforts of Operation Rescue. They complain that protest marches and civil disobedience are unbecoming for Christians. But the real embarrassment to Christianity is those who do nothing—followers of Christ who are silent on critical issues. Martin Luther's words are relevant to this point:

> If I profess with the loudest voice and clearest exposition every portion of the truth of God except precisely that little point which the world and the devil are at that moment attacking, I am not confessing Christ, however boldly I may be professing Christ. Where the battle rages, there the loyalty of the soldier is proved, and to be steady on all the battlefield besides, is mere flight and disgrace if he flinches at that point.

Some also accuse rescuers on the grounds that civil disobedience is called for only when government compels Christians to do evil or physically prohibits them from following God's commands. But rescuers *do* meet this Biblical standard because the government is prohibiting obedience to one of God's highest laws—to love our neighbor as ourselves. The unborn baby is as much our neighbor as the lonely fellow next door or the elderly lady up the street. It is a high form of love to save a helpless child from senseless and brutal murder, even if it takes personal sacrifice to accomplish that (see John 15:12, 13).

If government law permitted doctors to pull 4,100 kids a day out of elementary school, march them onto the hospital lawn, and brutally mutilate their bodies, would Christians stand by and say, "We must obey the governing authorities. They are God's ordained instruments. We cannot intervene"? Of course not! Christians have patiently sought an end to abortion in our land for over eighteen years. We have prayed and worked tirelessly, using every legal means available. Yet the murder rate continues—*one and a half million per year!* A Christian must participate in civil disobedience when all other options have failed. Sometimes full obedience to God can be carried out in no other way, and we must be prepared to accept the consequences of such action.

Others criticize rescuers on the grounds that they are stirring up passions which may result in anarchy. But when a heinous crime is being committed, passions should be stirred! Further, *Roe v. Wade* has already made anarchy a rule of law. Today a doctor can walk into a hospital room and perform a C-section to save a six-month-old preemie. He may use heroic measures and incur tremendous costs if the parent wants that child to live. But that same doctor can then go into a room across the hall and brutally terminate a healthy six-month-old unborn baby simply because the mother doesn't want him or her to live. The Supreme Court has granted the general citizenry the power to make such life and death decisions. This is barbaric! Husbands and wives, parents and children must make this a topic of urgent prayer and of whatever protest or activism God guides them to practice. We are at war, and the lives of millions are at stake.

Others opposing rescue operations point out that the rescuers are violating trespass laws by blocking access to abortion clinics. If we saw a woman being raped or a child being molested on private property with a No Trespassing sign on it, would we ignore the greater crime in order to comply with the lesser? The implications for abortion are obvious.

Of course, rescues of this nature may become moot in the near future if the abortion pill, RU-486, is legalized in America. That is why Christians, in addition to protest rallies, hot lines, sidewalk counseling, and rescue operations, must provide a clear moral vision as to why unborn life ought to be protected. Otherwise, even if we succeed in reversing current laws, a certain amount of women will seek back-alley abortions or use RU-486.

While Christians should vehemently denounce such abuses as violence, vigilantism, sensationalism, and sheer dramatics, we cannot dismiss all civil disobedience. We may not feel led to be rescuers, opting for more conventional tactics. But we must not add to the problems rescuers already face (police brutality, unsympathetic judges, legal red tape) with uninformed criticisms of their efforts. It is our privilege to use whatever pro-life method(s) God puts on our heart, but we must be careful to not undermine the efforts of those who are laying their reputations and careers on the line. Instead, it would be good for all members of our families, from the youngest to the oldest, to honor rescuers' convictions, speak well of them, and most of all pray for them.

Also, the Christian community must continue to offer realistic alternatives to pregnant woman. In the early years after *Roe v. Wade*, women were being counseled that abortion was wrong, but were offered little beyond that. As the years passed, the evangelical church has become more organized and now often refers women to local crisis pregnancy centers and adoption services. Volunteers are continually needed to staff these centers and to provide a whole range of desperately-needed assistance. For information on how you can help an existing crisis pregnancy center or start your own, call or write:

Christian Action Council
701 W. Broad Street
Suite 405
Falls Church, VA 22046
(703) 237-2100

Since the Supreme Court's decision on *Webster v. Reproductive Health Services* in 1989, the abortion issue has been returned to the

Faithful in a Fallen Culture

states. Thus Christian activists in state governments are needed more than ever. If enough Christians are willing to get involved, we can be effective in influencing state lawmakers to revamp or overturn pro-abortion legislation. Also, with the appointment of David Souter to the Supreme Court, and the Louisiana Pro-life Law, *Roe* stands a chance of being overturned in our land's highest court. This ought to be frequently mentioned in family prayers.

Guiding Principle:
Radical Christians make a clear stand for the value of life and will do whatever God asks to fight the abortion holocaust and other such evils. This must be seen as all-out war against the spiritual forces of wickedness and must be fought in God's way and with God's weapons.

CALLED TO WAR

To be radical Christians is to be warriors for the Lord Jesus Christ. We have not been summoned to lives of comfort and ease. We have been called to take up our cross and follow Jesus into battle. That battle includes Christian activism and the fight for righteousness through spreading the salt of morality. Either we are promoting or hurting His cause (see Matthew 12:30). It is not enough to say, "I'm holding my ground." Jesus commands us to not only defend what we have, but to attack the fortresses of evil. It is not enough to say, "Satan has not defeated me." We must go into his territory and conquer new turf. We must take Jesus' often overlooked words to heart here: "... on this rock I will build my church, *and the gates of Hades will not overcome it*" (Matthew 16:18). Are we attacking the gates of the enemy? There is only one way to do this—through relentless spiritual warfare. Such warfare necessitates personal action and involvement on the part of every true believer in the church and in our families.

RECOMMENDED READING

I would especially encourage the reading of two key volumes on the matters discussed in this chapter:

Kingdoms in Conflict by Charles Colson (Zondervan)

Suffer the Little Children by Mark Belz (Crossway Books)

SIX

Radical Christian Living, Part I

We now turn our attention to various issues concerning family life in relation to a sanctified and orderly lifestyle. Society is continually trying to change our thinking about the family. Departure from the Biblical blueprint for the family has been tragic for many. It will take more than a boy's finger to plug a ten-foot hole in the dike of family living. The recasting of Biblical models has been radical, and so must be the Christian response.

We will look carefully at several key areas in which we must regain radical Christian commitment in daily living, some more obvious than others, but all equally strategic.

AVOID ATTITUDE DECAY

Without necessary moral precautions, family attitudes are unavoidably affected by our culture. We live in a world in which pessimism and chronic complaining is rampant, and we easily absorb these into our minds and spirits. It's easier to pull someone down than to pull them up. Negativity unleashes such undesirable results as deflated self-worth, depressive attitudes, loss of closeness, argumentation, marital conflict, regressive health, children that continually fuss and are critical of each other, and general familial demoralization.

People in our society complain about a thousand and one things: their job, politics, the church, weather, moral decline, the threat of war, interest rates, pollution, the poisoning of our food chain, and on and on. Allowing chronic complaining in our presence reaps regrettable consequences. Eventually we will begin reflecting these same inauspicious attitudes in our own relationships. Such is clearly not the will of God.

Far too many Christians have inadequate defenses against the critical spirit of others. Hence they are easily influenced by and succumb to negative attitudes. Your family enjoys being around you when you are cheerful and enthusiastic, but no family likes living with a grouch. It is better to have a sunny smile than an unpleasant frown or a disposition that gives the impression you were baptized in vinegar.

Pessimism and negativity are often thrust upon us in situations we cannot avoid—at work, school, or through friends and relatives—and thus we are constantly being conditioned to think the way the world thinks and to see life the way the world sees it. Therefore, it is imperative that we and our families learn how to refuse pessimism. I am not suggesting that we mask reality or have a head-in-the-sand approach to life. But I am suggesting that we promote an environment where positive attitudes can flourish while simultaneously limiting our exposure to unnecessary negativity. We will now discuss ten ways to accomplish this.

First, we can make a list of encouraging Scriptures in a personal notebook, or invest in a Bible promise book.

Second, we can take time to encourage and build up our families. We can build a hedge of optimism around them with positive comments and loving remarks. Criticizing our families is like stabbing at our automobile tires with an ice pick. Sooner or later such an action will stop our forward mobility.

Third, we can seek friendships with positive, upbeat Christians. There are many such Christian men and women with whom we can cultivate close friendships. "He who walks with the wise grows wise, but a companion of fools suffers harm" (Proverbs 13:20).

Fourth, we can fill each day with spiritually uplifting Christian music or praise tapes. We can play this music by our bathroom sink, in the kitchen, in the car. Three tape clubs that I personally enjoy are:

Integrity's Hosanna! Music
P.O. Box Z
Mobile, AL 36616

Benson Music
1415 Lake Drive S.E.
Grand Rapids, MI 49506
(800) 727-1309

Maranatha! Music
P.O. 31050
Laguna Hills, CA 92654-1050
(800) 245-7664

Fifth, We can try to be enthusiastic in every task we undertake. This is one of the best testimonies we can give to show our love for God and the life He has given us. Dale Carnegie said, "Act enthusiastic and you will be enthusiastic." Who has more to be joyful about than born-again Christians?

Sixth, we can set up a program of regular exercise. Top physicians all across the country agree that regular and proper exercise is critical to good health. We each only have one body, so we better take care of it.

Seventh, we can be liberal with our praise of others. We should give what we like to receive ourselves. If we enjoy positive, complimentary remarks, we should generously distribute them to those around us. Kind remarks have a delightful boomerang effect.

Eighth, we should not spend a great deal of time with people who have no sense of Christian purpose in their lives. Many people lead merry-go-round lives; they spend energy going around and around, but their life is going nowhere. They provide other people with a few passing moments of pleasure, but leave no lasting spiritual effect on the world in which they live. Hanging around people like that will distort our vision and our purpose for being here.

Ninth, we can get all unnecessary negative data out of our lives. Newspapers and the evening television news often bring us feelings of fear, anxiety, and depression. Yes, we need to be informed, but we need balance here, as in all areas of our lives.

Tenth, we can put an immediate damper on the critical remarks and pessimism of others. The minute others start harping and carping, we should speak to them about it—kindly and politely if we can, boldly and vigorously if they give us no other choice. We also should not allow our acceptance of someone else's pessimism to imply approval. Jesus had a sympathetic ear, but nowhere do we find Him voluntarily listening to the negativity of others.

Tom Hopkins, a best-selling author and renowned speaker on motivation and success, refers to the handling of pessimism as a sanitation job. He warns, "Avoid unnecessary exposure to the germs that pessimists carry, disinfect yourself after exposure to one of them...."[1] To keep our effectiveness for Christ from being impeded, we need to learn how to graciously avoid those who want to waste our time with chronic complaining.

Let me summarize with an analogy. Pessimism or negativity is bilgewater, and our lives are like ships. All ships leak a little, but that's no problem, as long as you keep pumping the bilgewater out.[2] We must learn how to keep our boats afloat. Consider the powerful words of Paul in Philippians 4:8: "whatever is true, whatever is noble, whatever is right, whatever is pure, whatever is lovely, whatever is admirable—if anything is excellent or praiseworthy—think about such things." We must constantly remind ourselves and our families of the meaning, value, and practical application of this Scripture.

Guiding Principle:
As radical Christians, it is imperative that we maintain an optimism and hope in the Lord, looking beyond the negativity of others and focusing on His purposes for us.

RESIST CULTURAL IMMODESTY

Christian families are salt when they maintain moral propriety. This is done by avoiding activities and environments where immorality can subtly become part of our mind-set and lifestyle. This is a tall spiritual order for family leadership, but one which radical Christians will work at continually.

In addition, Christian families will teach the value of and personally engage in modest attire. Though immodest dress has become an acceptable way of life in our culture, Christian men and women need not—in fact, must not—participate in the trend. Christian modesty and respect for others, not style, fashion, or fad, should determine the clothes we wear.

Dressing modestly has several advantages.
- It reminds us who we are—followers of Christ.
- It enhances our self-respect.
- It shows respect and sensitivity for those around us.
- It frees us from the fashion fads of the day.
- It helps others see us as persons rather than objects.
- It lessens chances of unwanted sexual advances.
- It has a positive effect on the kind of friends we attract.

Outside of unwholesome video and cable TV viewing, the most glaring form of culturally-accepted immodesty is the attire worn at public swimming and sunbathing facilities. Radical Christians will not wear such attire. Also, modern exercise apparel is designed to be sexually suggestive. Though Christians cannot avoid going out in public, they can choose where they go and when and may choose to avoid co-ed exercise clubs and aerobic centers. The follower of Christ must always be guided by moral propriety. "But among you there must not be even a hint of sexual immorality, or of any kind of impurity, or of greed, because these are improper for God's holy people" (Ephesians 5:3).

There is a great deal of the old Adam within each of us; none of us is immune to lust, temptation, and sin. We must beware of the schemes of the enemy to discredit the gospel in our lives. We must also clearly explain godly reasoning on these matters to our children so they understand why we resist cultural immodesty. How we dress each and every day can promote modesty as well as offer a Christian witness to the world.

Guiding Principle:

We must select and wear clothes that will not cause another man or woman to stumble. Could we wear these clothes before the Lord Jesus Christ without embarrassment?

Christians must take precautions against all forms of moral impropriety. God is righteous and wants His people to be righteous too. Hence, the radical Christian family will go the extra mile to "Avoid every kind of evil" (1 Thessalonians 5:22) and thus protect their minds and hearts. There are many places radical Christian families will not go, many things they will not do, say, or condone. They will be careful concerning what they allow themselves to see, touch, hear, or read. The secular world will not understand this and will accuse us of being social isolationists or perhaps worse. Less committed Christians might see our stand on moral righteousness as being overbearing or legalistic. So be it. The fruit of our families' lifestyle will be evident soon enough. Whatever we do, we must not gamble with our family's moral purity.

RETHINK MODERN DATING PRACTICES

As a purely Western phenomenon, dating is another cultural practice that needs to be reexamined by radical Christians. For many boys and girls steady dating has led to immorality. Some evidence suggests that the earlier young people start dating, the earlier they start fornicating. The research findings of Brent Miller (Utah State University) and Terrence Olsen (Brigham Young University) reveals the following correlation:

> The younger a girl begins to date, the more likely she is to have sex before graduating from high school. It is also true of girls and boys who go steady in the ninth grade. Of girls who begin dating at twelve, 91 percent had sex before graduation—compared to 56 percent who dated at thirteen, 53 percent who dated at fourteen, 40 percent who dated at fifteen, and 20 percent who dated at sixteen. Of boys with a ninth-grade steady, 70 percent said that they'd had sex compared to 60 percent of girls. Of boys who dated occasionally as freshmen, 52 percent had sex compared to 35 percent of girls.[3]

To help you visualize the repercussions of early dating, examine the chart "Early Dating Promotes Fornication," found in Appendix D. We must ask, what is the purpose of dating at an early age? Early teens certainly are not planning to get married. Nor are they physically or emotionally ready to set guidelines for themselves, especially when they are alone for hours at a time with the opposite sex. The temptations in such situations, even for Christians, are just too great. Prolonged periods of intimate emotional sharing in an unprotected environment will in most cases lead to physical intimacy. Steady dating tempts teenagers to engage in sexual activity long before they are ready to enter into engagement and marriage. Christian parents must take appropriate firm but loving action to protect their teens from falling into moral impurity.

Guiding Principle:
To help our sons and daughters avoid lust and impurity, we must not allow them to go out alone with the opposite sex in unsupervised situations. We should help them avoid any setting or social environment that fosters or abets sin.

We need to recognize that *Christians can socialize without dating.* Christian teenagers can spend time with godly friends without facing the moral temptations of steady dating. *Socializing* means being with Christian peers for the purposes of fellowship, companionship, and fun, with an underlying motive of reaffirming Christian convictions and strengthening faith in Jesus Christ. Obviously these goals are more important than merely being together for physical closeness or pleasure.

Christian parents are responsible to teach their children appropriate guidelines for socialization. The first rule of thumb is, *we must not permit our sons or daughters to go out alone for hours at a time.* That is, socializing should be carried out in groups. A child may ask, "Mom, Dad, don't you trust me?" We can counter, "No . . . I don't even trust myself." We can explain to our children that even Christians must deal with the wickedness in their own hearts. C. H. Spurgeon once described man's heart as a tinderbox ready to be set aflame by the smallest spark. We are all susceptible to the temptations of our flesh and must take protective steps to guard ourselves. Paul told Timothy to "Flee the evil desires of youth" (2 Timothy 2:22), and this is excellent advice for us all.

Our culture is so permeated with sexual stimuli that it doesn't take much to get someone's motor running. Sometimes the only way to handle temptation is to flee from the environment where it is strongest. Joseph ran from his own youthful lust when an immoral opportunity presented itself in Potiphar's house. We should teach our children this lesson.

Children should be taught early that the best socializing takes place within the family context. If your fifteen-year-old daughter likes a young man, let her invite him over to the house for the afternoon. Or they can go bowling or picnicking with the family. Or they can go out in threes, and she can take along a brother or sister or a friend. One advantage to spending time together at home is that we need to reestablish within our culture respect for and interaction with the entire family. Building activities around the family will also provide built-in chaperoning that helps keep young emotions within proper bounds.

Second, we must *build and maintain a rapport with our children that encourages them to be accountable to us for their actions.* They should be taught, from a young age on up, the importance of accountability to parents and pastors. Many young people today, when asked by a concerned parent or friend about their moral purity, will retort, "It is none of your business." While on the campaign trail, a recent candidate for United States President was asked by a reporter about his marital fidelity. He indignantly responded, "I don't think that's any of your business!" If they had asked him, "Are you an embezzler?" or "Are you on crack?" he probably would have answered. But there is a mind-set among people today that views sexual moral questions in an entirely different light, as an invasion of privacy. This is individualistic paganism.

If our sons or daughters profess to be blood-bought followers of Jesus Christ and someone asks them about their moral purity, they should answer honestly. A Christian's life should be an open book, not a locked box. In fact, Christian accountability must be practiced by every member of the family.

Third, *we must realize that concocting ground rules is not enough to overcome the temptations and the lack of safeguards that typical dating entails.* To send an alcoholic into a package liquor store and tell him to only buy Coke is to invite violation. To tell a youngster, "don't use drugs" while letting him go to a party where drug use is the norm is begging for trouble. He can't help but be influenced by his environment. Hanging around in an immoral environment led the godly Samson to fornicate and ultimately caused his demise. Instead of worrying about your children's moral purity on a date, why allow them to be in that kind of a situation in the first place? Why not teach your teenager a whole new way of thinking?

One of the hardest things for a teenager to contend with while trying to live the radical Christian life is peer pressure. If our children are committed to a Biblical standard for behavior toward the opposite sex, they will face intense ridicule and mockery. This is one of many reasons why home education has such important merit. If home schooling is not possible, we should at least strongly consider putting our children in a Christian school.

Socializing in college and beyond also demands controls. Allowed free rein, sensual desires quickly master even the most sincere Christians. For this reason engaged couples need to beware of becoming physically intimate prior to marriage. Too much time spent together in privacy or semi-privacy can lead to a fall.

Also, as parents we must teach our children, at an early age, the importance of socializing *with Christians*. Young men and women often rationalize away the Scriptural principle of not dating non-Christians. Below are some common excuses youngsters use. We must be careful to not allow such thinking to enter our reasoning or our children's.

> "He does not claim to follow Jesus because he doesn't want to be a hypocrite."
> "He doesn't claim Christ as Savior, but he is a real sweet guy."
> "He will become a believer when I tell him it's a requirement for marriage."
> "He is a very open-minded person. I'll witness to him on our dates. I'm sure sooner or later he will become a Christian."
> "He promised me he would start going to church after we are married. He definitely wants our children to go to church."

"He had a bad experience with a church some time ago. With time he will get it all straightened out and start attending church again."

"He is more of a gentleman than most Christians I know."

"Apart from religion, we have almost everything in common."

"We really love each other; we will work out the rest in time."

"When he gets away from his parents, he will surely become a Christian."

"If I keep my dating standards too high, I'll never get married."

Spiritual oneness in Christ is the basis for the deepest and most lasting relationships, especially in marriage. Scripture clearly states: "Do not be yoked together with unbelievers. For what do righteousness and wickedness have in common? Or what fellowship can light have with darkness? What harmony is there between Christ and Belial? What does a believer have in common with an unbeliever?" (2 Corinthians 6:14, 15). If it's wrong to marry an unbeliever, it's also wrong to date an unbeliever.

There are several practical things we parents can do to help promote purity in our sons or daughters. First, we must encourage them to develop godly companions, praying with them for the right peers with whom to socialize.

Second, we can teach them that impure suggestions often catch conscientious Christians off-guard and bring temptation at times we don't expect it. We must give them ammunition to fight off the enemy, carefully going over key Scriptures with them.[4]

Third, and this must start early, it is imperative that we be the first in their life to give them sex education. It is much better for knowledge about physical intimacy to come from parents than from strangers. Many of today's sex education courses contain harmful and un-Scriptural concepts. Remember that sex education is partly basic biology, but the rest is pure commentary. Both the instruction and the commentary should come from parents. There are several good books you can use. Write or call:

Teen Aid
1330 N. Calispel
Spokane, WA 99201
(509) 466-8679

Project Respect
Box 97
Golf, IL 60029

Why Wait?
Box 1000
Dallas, TX 75221
(214) 907-1000
[Why Wait is distinctively Christian]

Project Respect also has a stunning video for teenagers entitled, *Everyone Is Not Doing It!* I also encourage every young man and woman to carefully read the book *Why Wait?* by Josh McDowell prior to ever spending time with the opposite sex. There is a parent guide as well.

Fathers, it is imperative that we teach our young sons how to fight off lust through Scripture memory, hard work, exercise, godly companions, and avoidance of tempting environments.

Conversely, mothers need to teach their young daughters how to maximize their feminine potential. This is best done by teaching them the priority of concentrating on inner beauty instead of outward appearance. Give them methods for improving both, including modesty, manners, proper use of makeup, purity, and honor. Carefully teach the Christian secret of true feminine beauty outlined in 1 Peter 3:3, 4.

Young adults living away from home must also be taught how to establish moral safeguards. Sons or daughters living in a college dormitory or apartment should be given this wise counsel: If you are planning to have a member of the opposite sex over, for your moral protection have a friend or roommate stay in the same room for the entire evening.; or if you go out, remember the importance of doing so with a group. There is ample opportunity for socialization through church functions or with other Christian friends. To do otherwise may risk moral impurity.

We must teach our children the basic rules for relating to the opposite sex and building moral safeguards. Should they confront situations that are not specifically mentioned in God's Word, here are four questions they can ask themselves to determine right or wrong:

- Will this situation be helpful to me physically . . . spiritually . . . mentally?
- Would it put me in the company of people who would be an unwholesome influence?
- Would it bring shame to the cross of Christ?
- Would it glorify God?

There is a proper time and place for dating, but when? I personally believe dating requires serious character evaluation, decision-making abilities, and emotional and spiritual maturity. Thus one should be out of high school before starting to date. A young man or woman is prepared for dating when he or she:

- Has prayed, seeking God's leading and guidance for the right person to date.
- Understands that the dating process should incorporate the same safeguards as socializing. He or she should try especially to avoid "alone time" and other opportunities for temptation, date in groups as much as possible, and "make not provision for the flesh" (Romans 13:14, KJV).
- Understands that parents should be involved from start to finish. Parental approval of his or her date, especially that of a godly father, demonstrates maturity and submission to proper authority. This is God's plan.

- Develops a strict dating schedule or agenda prior to leaving on his or her date and is accountable to his or her parents (or some other godly authority figure).
- Under God's guidance has worked out a set of Scriptural dating standards and goals for himself or herself.
- Understands that the foremost purpose of dating is to develop a oneness of spirit, which when achieved can be the basis of engagement and marriage. He or she should center on relationship-building that is spiritual, emotional, and social instead of physical.
- And, above all else, remembers to date *only* born-again Christians with the same moral convictions as himself or herself.

SEVEN

Radical Christian Living, Part II

Jesus Christ calls us to a high plane of spiritual living, and obedience to Him will impact a number of practical areas of our lives.

REVERSE THE SHRINKING FAMILY TREND

It seems as though someone has put out a contract on the stork, because the liberal outcry against large families has succeeded in altering societal thinking. The average number of children nationwide is approximately 1.8 per household. Hence we have become a nation that cannot even replace itself. Marching to a constant drumbeat of misinformation, feminists, world resource alarmists, family planning consultants, and population control fanatics have succeeded in befuddling the facts. As a result, many young couples are confused about the subject.

"Limit your family" reasoning has even invaded the Christian community. Young couples afraid of the "terrors" of unrestrained childbearing now find their minds poisoned with a litany of "can'ts." What does the Bible have to say about limiting our family's size?

Nowhere in Scripture does God issue regulations on keeping a family small, but numerous Scriptures do command us to have children. The very first of these was given to Adam and Eve shortly after creation—"Be fruitful and increase in number; fill the earth and subdue it" (Genesis 1:28). The same command was given to Noah in Genesis 9:1. God considered (and still considers) children a blessing and not a curse, despite what many today would have us think.

Some might object, "But those commands were given to an uninhabited planet. Naturally God would want people then to reproduce and fill the earth." True, but in numerous other places God clearly put His divine stamp of approval upon childbearing for all generations. In Psalm 127 Solomon, in inspired wisdom, gives this insight: "Behold, *children are a gift of the Lord; the fruit of the womb is a reward.* Like arrows in the hand of a warrior, so are the children of one's youth. How *blessed is the man whose quiver is full of them; they shall not be ashamed*" (v. 3-5, NASB). Notice that children are called "a gift," and the couple that has them is called "blessed." (Note: A full quiver usually meant anything from six to twelve arrows, but this illustration is meant to be figurative, not literal.)

In 1 Timothy 5:14 wives are specifically told to "have children" and "to manage their homes." Children have always been considered a sign of divine blessing upon God-fearing believers. Historically the number of children a couple had was never limited or predesignated, and nowhere in Scripture are God's people commanded to artificially restrain or control childbirth. Throughout Bible days the raising up of a godly family was considered a most admirable pursuit.

Do the "can'ts" our minds have been bombarded with have any merit? Below are refutations of seven common arguments against trusting God to give us as large families as He desires.

Phobia #1: "I Can't Afford Children"

Says who? Statistical data on how expensive it is to raise a child in modern America is often riddled with inaccuracies, false assumptions, and obvious biases. While trying to reinforce the imperative of a controlled birth rate, these same studies neglect to mention the child-rearing effectiveness of parents who are less economically privileged. In fact, lower-income families have defied the socioeconomic odds for centuries. The reason is simple—children's material needs are minimal. They can grow up happy, healthy and godly with far less than our materialistically satiated culture would lead us to believe. Don't be conned by the economic prevarications which are responsible for the growing societal prevalence of DINKS (Double Income–No Kids). God is a God of abundant supply, and He who blesses us with children will certainly help us feed and clothe them.

Phobia #2: "We Can't Control That Many Children"

Sociologists claim that people become increasingly hostile, aggressive and uncontrollable as their numbers increase on the globe. While this theory may prove true with rats, I don't think home life can be compared to a rat cage. Properly raised children are not the wild, unruly animals they are often depicted to be. Children want to love and be loved. Some may go through a temporary stage of rebellion, but that's a far cry from being malicious, uncontrollable juvenile delinquents. Parents who are liberal with love and firm guidance raise children who display godly character traits of self-restraint and self-discipline (Galatians 5:22, 23). Children who are properly taught don't have to be controlled—they control themselves.

Children reflect their parents. If the parents act obstreperous and undignified, so will the children. If parents are courteous and well-mannered, this will manifest itself in the children's attitude and behavior as well.

Phobia #3: "A Large Family Spells Death to My Career"

A professional, out-of-the-home career for a married woman is not always the greener pasture the college textbooks describe it to be. Why do you think the work world is dubbed a "rat race"? Is it really *fulfilling* for a mother to shove her innocent child into day-care and grind out a 9-to-5 job, thus achieving the dubious benefits of rebellious children, increased marital conflict, and stress-related maladies?

It is more laudable to serve than to be served. Which is more service-oriented—raising a family of godly children who will have a positive impact on society, or chasing after one's own individualistic interests? The most noble and worthy professions on earth are motherhood and fatherhood. If a woman's career and her children are mutually exclusive, the wife should hang her hopes on the one which is more honorable and far more fulfilling—the raising of a godly family.

Phobia #4: "Our Marriage Can't Stand the Strain"
Really? Would a loving God command married couples to be fruitful and multiply, knowing that obedience would cause their union to fall apart at the emotional seams? Will not God give moms and dads the strength to look after His "gift?" Properly carried out, family life will strengthen, not strain, a marriage. A home with several children will certainly at times have its challenges, but it also has its own joys.

Phobia #5: "I Don't Want to Raise Children in a Corrupt World"
If Noah would have thought the same way, there would have been no children to carry on the human race. God sent His own Son into a world filled with paganism, materialism, immorality and government-sponsored infanticide (under Herod). We must realize that the power of Christ is greater than the evil of this world (1 John 4:4). Relinquishing our duty as salt and light is not an option. The hope of the world lies in Christian influence, and the future of Christian influence lies with Christian children.

Phobia #6: "Unrestrained Childbirth Ruins a Woman's Health"
Granted, there are medical considerations if a woman is bearing her first child in her late thirties or early forties. But there can also be health risks due to the cumulative effect of being on the Pill for years. Moreover, contrary to common assumption, there is a higher incidence of ovarian and uterine cancer among childless women than among mothers.[1]

On the flipside, other research seems to indicate a correlation between multiple births and cancer prevention. *The American Journal of Epidemiology* published a study which found "a strong and highly significant inverse association between the number of full-term pregnancies and the risk of breast cancer."[2] In fact, there is "a stronger protective effect with increasing number of children."[3] Hence, a mother of one runs a higher risk of breast cancer than a mother of two or more. Interestingly enough, only full-term pregnancies reduce the risk of breast cancer. Obviously, Planned Parenthood will never give out this information.

Phobia #7: "We Will Have a Population Explosion and Use Up All Our Natural Resources"

For decades demographers and alarmists have been projecting geometric population growth and have been using frightening and panic-producing metaphors (for example, "population explosion" and "population bomb"). One of the lead spokesmen for this movement was Paul R. Ehrlich. In my college days Ehrlich's book *The Population Bomb* was required reading in freshman biology. Ehrlich's theory was that "the earth simply does not have the resources to support an ever increasing population density. Therefore, we must limit the number of children born into this world."

Baby boomers have been heavily indoctrinated with this theory, as well as with its intimidating solution—Zero Population Growth. We have been told that overpopulation hangs like an ominous cloud over our resource-depleted world, daring mankind to step beyond the point of no return; if we do, a cloud will descend on mankind to inflict mass starvation, disease and other unspeakable horrors.

However, the theories of population bombers have never proven true, and their fears have been shown to be groundless. Paul Ehrlich predicted "hundreds of millions" would starve in the 1970s due to overpopulation. They didn't. For one thing, new technology keeps finding methods of higher productivity and of stretching natural resources. Also, the population density of the world is nowhere near reaching a critical zone. Biologist Francis P. Felice points out that:

... all the people in the world could be put into the state of Texas, forming one giant city with a population density less than that of many existing cities, and leaving the rest of the world empty. Each man, woman, and child in the 1984 world population could be given more than 1,500 square feet of land space in such a city (the average home in the United States ranges between 1,400 and 1,800 square feet). If one-third of the space of this city were devoted to parks and one-third to industry, each family could still occupy a single-story dwelling of average U.S. size.[4]

Obviously, population alarmists who tell us we are running out of space are not giving us all the facts. In her book *The War Against Population*, Dr. Jacqueline Kasun gives this assessment of the depleting-resources falsehood:

Resources, far from being limited, are abounding. No more than 1 to 3 percent of the earth's ice-free land area is occupied by human beings, less than one-ninth is used for agricultural purposes. Eight times, and perhaps as much as twenty-two times, the world's present population could support itself at the present standard of living, using present technology; and this leaves half the earth's land surface open to wildlife and conservation areas. The ubiquitous and overworked visitor from Mars would be astonished to discover that the earth planet, with its resources barely touched, its yawning spaces, and its human fertility rapidly declining, is in the throes of a panic about overpopulation.[5]

The one thing progeny controllers don't include in their overpopulation equation is that God is still in control. Scripture does not say, "Be fruitful and multiply until you think the world borders on overpopulation." It simply tells us to be fruitful and leave the rest in His hands. In Biblical days a large and growing population was considered a blessing to a nation, and a shrinking population was considered ruinous (Proverbs 14:28).

Unfortunately, a shrinking population is what we now have. It is becoming crystal-clear that instead of geometric population growth, the Western world is witnessing a *decreasing population trend due to below-replacement fertility*. While primarily a Western problem, even some Third-World countries such as Indonesia and Brazil have declining birth rates. As with the frightful warnings of population growth, population decrease proceeds geometrically, not arithmetically. Hence the grave concern in the demographic community now is not population explosion but geometric *population implosion*.[6]

Concerns about low fertility surfaced publicly on the 1988 campaign trail of GOP presidential hopefuls Pat Robertson and Jack Kemp. Now that the issue has come out of the closet, it promises to gather more steam as the threat of population deficiency becomes increasingly evident. Underpopulation is a serious crisis which must be addressed. Yet, we have a whole generation of baby boomers convinced of the virtues of population zero.

Ben J. Wattenberg, senior fellow at the American Enterprise Institute, has published a book entitled *The Birth Dearth*, which deals powerfully with this very issue. Wattenberg pinpoints two main problems of underpopulation: lowered economic demand and a graying society. Addressing the *economic* implications Wattenberg gives this analogy:

> A Birth Dearth not only provides fewer workers, it provides fewer buyers. Consider the housing industry. It is triggered by young adults buying first homes. But from 1990 to 2000, the number of Americans age 25-34 will shrink by 18 percent due to the low fertility rates of the 1960s and the 1970s. Moreover, Birth Dearth fertility patterns mean more old people relative to the population as a whole. They die, leaving vacant residences, further shrinking the need for new housing. The new housing industry makes up 10 percent of the GNP. That sector is due for tough times.[7]

The impact can be further seen by the chart in Appendix A ("U.S. Fertility Freefall"). Another chart ("Long-range Picture of Fertility

Slide") shows population projections for the future at current rates of fertility (1.815 total fertility rate). If we have a TFR of 1.6, as some are projecting, U.S. population will fall dramatically in the next century. Another area of economic impact will be the crippling or even bankruptcy of the Social Security Trust Fund. Says Wattenberg:

> In 1985, there were 145 million people of working age in the U.S. to pay Social Security taxes for 29 million elderly. That's a ratio of 5 producers for 1 retiree. But in 2035, as the Baby Boomers retire and the Baby Boomers diminish the labor force, the ratio will be only two and a half to one.
>
> Sooner or later, Social Security "goes broke" unless something changes. That can happen fairly quickly if Social Security absorbs Medicare liabilities, or somewhat later, if not. Where will the extra money come from? It will be hard to raise through bigger taxes on the slender legions of the Birth Dearth. There won't be enough of them to pay what is needed for the elderly to take advantage of the new life-extending, health-extending-expensive-medical technology. In a pay-as-you-go Social Security system such as ours, the working-age population must put babies as well as money into the pot. Not enough babies equals trouble.[8]

Left unabated, the specter of an aging United States has serious ramifications. Is the American eagle turning out to be an ostrich? "A Rapidly Graying America," another chart in Appendix A, gives us a frightening picture.

The size of a nation's population per se—not just its troop levels—directly affects its military power. Wattenberg supports this contention with the projected shrinkage rate of modern democracies. For example, in 1950 the population of the free world comprised about 22 percent of the world population. Today it is about 15 percent. By 2030 our present trend will leave us with 9 percent. By the end of the next century we will be down to a minuscule 5 percent (see the chart "Western Share of World Population"). The question then arises, can the

Western world still dominate when its human influence comprises only 5 percent of the global population? And if it doesn't, who will? Communist-bloc nations continue to have a total fertility rate of 2.3 births per woman compared to our 1.8. That's 28 percent higher than Western democracies. Underpopulation spawns a subtle *military danger*, one which is inseparably connected to the brute economic production of the United States.

> Larger populations can build more easily the infrastructure that supports national defense. And attaining technological leadership requires a large critical mass of scientists. Only a large consumer market can support much broad-based, industrial scientific innovation, which often spins off into the military field (as happened in the U.S. with Star Wars technology.) Only a large society can tax its people enough to finance major research and development directly for the military (such as Star Wars) or build and then sustain the monumental weapons of modern warfare (such as aircraft-carrier battle groups). And, of course, a large society makes it easier to provide the manpower for the armed services.[9]

In addition to decreasing fertility rates, the Western world has other contributors to its alarming population freefall—including continued abortion and the specter of ever-rising AIDS mortality. The pre-natal murder rate in America is currently 1.6 million per year (about one every 19.7 seconds). The United States has a much higher annual abortion rate—about 28 for every 1,000 women between the ages of fifteen and forty-four—than other Western nations. In Sweden, by contrast, the rate is 18 per 1,000.[10] Though the moral consideration surrounding the origin of life is the primary reason for opposing abortion, abortion also has many negative social repercussions, including physical peril to the mother, risk to future conception, and emotional trauma. Unfortunately, according to Dr. Irvin Cusher of UCLA Medical School, 98 percent of all abortions are done because women "do not wish to be pregnant at this particular time."[11] In other words, the majority are performed merely for convenience sake. That's is a telling commentary on a society that claims to be concerned about human rights violations. Abortion has become society's out-of-sight, out-of-mind "cure" for a deep moral and spiritual dilemma. In the meantime, the combined effect of abortion and a lower fertility rate compound the problem of underpopulation.

AIDS mortality is also a growing factor. The astronomical growth of AIDS infection in the United States portends more lives lost than in a major war. AIDS is more dangerous and has far greater capacity for rapid spread than any other previous epidemic which has devastated large sections of humanity. Unfortunately, government under-reporting of the number of HIV-infected people keeps the average citizen from having a clear view of how widespread the epidemic is or how quickly it is growing. Even at reported rates, the AIDS pandemic will mushroom and contribute further to America's dwindling population, power, and economic muscle.

After the smoke of rhetoric and misinformation clears, it becomes apparent that having larger families would be a boon to our country and to Christianity in particular. Even apart from the obedience factor of being "fruitful and increas[ing] in number" (Genesis 1:28), Christians can have a powerful spiritual impact numerically. Mary Pride presents an interesting scenario:

> Let's say that Christians are 20 percent of the U.S. population. If each Christian family had six children, and the humanists, feminists, and others kept on having an average of one (which is realistic, considering how they feel about fruitful heterosexual marriage), then in twenty years there would be sixty of us for every forty of them. In forty years *90 percent of America would be Christian!* That is *without* outside evangelism. All we'd have to do would be to have children and raise them for Christ. Even if Christians were only 2 percent of the population (which I think is more accurate), then in two generations, at the reproduction rates

I already mentioned, we would be over 40 percent of the population.[12]

Children are gifts from God, and a woman's body is the vehicle for that blessing. When Paul says, "women shall be preserved through the bearing of children" (1 Timothy 2:15, NASB), he means that childbearing is one of the great natural functions of a saved woman. Women who profess godliness yet deliberately contravene God's divine purpose of bearing children are ignoring a God-given privilege and responsibility. (Marital partners unable to conceive for medical reasons is another matter entirely.) Contrary to feminist rhetoric, a woman's body is not her own—it belongs to God.

A growing number of couples today delay parenthood or unnecessarily place restrictions on the size of their family. Over the past ten years there has been a sizable increase in the number of American women not giving birth until thirty-five or older. Like other children, last-chance kids are loved and appreciated when they arrive. However, their growing number reflects cultural attitudes which place a higher emphasis on selfish independence, establishing a career, and completing formal education than on having a family. While putting off children can seemingly be favorable to the parents' timetable, it is not always in a child's best interest. For example, studies show that last-chance children are beleaguered with a higher incidence of loneliness and increased fears about parental death.[13]

It is clear that a major part of God's will for Christian husbands and wives concerns procreative activity. Men and women joined in the bonds of wedlock can contribute to the strength of God's spiritual army on earth. Godly parents who are willing to raise devoted Christian children can help change the country, indeed the world. The Bible says that a man who fears the Lord will have children who "will be mighty in the land" (Psalm 112:2). When Christian attitudes toward family size begin to mirror that of unbelieving society, something is very wrong. Christians all across our great land should reconsider the privilege of having and raising large families.

There is no doubt about it—*families flourish when they are obedient to God's will and see children as the blessings they really are.*

Guiding Principle:
Radical Christian parents trust God to determine the size of their families and welcome children as special gifts from a loving Lord.

EIGHT

Radical Christian Living, Part III

In this chapter we want to continue looking at some areas of American life that need serious reevaluation by committed Christians. Taking a righteous and determined stand is not easy, but it is necessary in order to maintain a sanctified and consistent lifestyle in which our families can flourish. We will now consider several additional areas in which we can return rational understanding and radical Christian commitment to daily living.

FACE THE TRUTH ABOUT BIRTH CONTROL

The time for ignorance about certain types of birth control must end. Some Christians unknowingly use abortifacient contraceptives such as the IUD and certain forms of the Pill. Women are usually warned about the risks of pregnancy and childbirth, but rarely are they warned about the risks from using these devices. The truth is, IUDs and certain compositions of the Pill do not prevent fertility but rather keep fertilized eggs from implanting and thus actually destroy human life.

The Pill is the most common contraceptive in use today. But in fact it has many risky side effects. It can cause infertility. Or, if a woman using it nevertheless conceives, the baby has an increased likelihood of medical problems. Some common medically-documented patient complaints among Pill users include: abdominal pain or swelling, abnormal menses or the absence of same, bloating, blood clots, breakthrough bleeding and spotting, breast discharge, breast pain, shortness of breath, chest pain, cramping, decrease in sex drive, depression, dizziness, fatigue, feelings of rejection or unrest, frequent urination, migraine headaches, hypoglycemia, insomnia, irritability, "morning sickness," pins-and-needles feelings, premenstrual syndrome, skin eruptions, vaginal discharge, varicose veins, vomiting, and many more.[1]

Unfortunately, these are the less perilous medical factors. A user also has a four to 9.5 times greater risk of thrombotic stroke, six times greater risk of developing hypertension (high blood pressure), and an increased risk of cervical neoplasms, vaginitis, vulvitis, moniliasis and trichomoniasis. Oral contraceptives have also been implicated in increased risk of myocardial infarction (heart attack).[2] It has long been suspected that women who used oral contraceptives before their first term birth had an increased risk of developing breast cancer before age forty-five.[3] Several new studies confirm this. One study of 2,133 women reported to the American Public Health Association these results: Pill users under age fifty face an average of 42 percent higher risk of breast cancer. Longer usage is linked to more cancer: 30 percent higher rate for those taking it less than four years, and a whopping 80 percent higher for more than four years.[4] This is a side of the Pill most women never hear about.

Like certain formulations of the Pill, IUDs are also an abortive device and have their own tragic record. Most IUDs have recently been yanked off the shelves due to litigation surrounding medical complications from their usage, though a few remain on the market. IUDs prevent intrauterine pregnancy but not extrauterine pregnancy. Hence, a woman can have a life-threatening ectopic pregnancy requiring emergency surgery. Other serious complications can also occur, including perforation of the cervix or uterus which could lead to intraperitoneal hemorrhage.[5] One of the more common complications of IUDs is pelvic inflammatory disease, which contributes greatly to infertility. Just three episodes of PID leaves 40 to 70 percent of IUD users infertile.[6]

Considering the risks and abortifacient nature of the Pill and IUDs, Christian women are advised to avoid usage altogether. More plausible alternatives are certainly available.

Guiding Principle:

As committed Christians and as parents, we owe it to God to do His will and to clearly and fully choose life.

RETHINK RETIREMENT

Another area radical Christians need to reappraise is the whole perception of one's retirement years. This subject may seem at first glance to be radically insignificant in comparison to the matters to which we have just given our attention. However, it warrants serious consideration.

We have been successfully indoctrinated with the notion that after the magic age of sixty-five we are ready for the pasture. Young workers are encouraged to start one or even several retirement plans to prepare for those "golden years." The many options can be confusing.

Often we hear people ruminate about their retirement dreams. "I look forward to placidly fishing in a cold, clear mountain lake beside my own cabin," says one. "Not I," says another; "I want to travel around the world and visit all the magnificent places I've read about in *National Geographic.*" There are as many dreams as there are people. But the goal is the same: to arrive at a point in life when one's remaining years can be spent in rest, relaxation and financial security. "I have paid my dues to society," the gray American says. "Now it's time for me to rest, relax, travel, and perhaps become a part-time, out-of-the-home entrepreneur." This is what retirement is all about . . . Or is it?

Do we retire because we want to or because we are led to believe that at age sixty-five our contribution diminishes? The very definition of the word *retire* means "to withdraw or retreat." But should the years that offer us our greatest freedom of mobility and financial security be a time of retreat? Should we view retirement as waning years of nonproductivity? Rather, should this not be a time of increased ministry?

The Western concept of retirement is a relatively recent phenomenon. It was not so in classical times.

> ... in earlier times the position of the aged was fixed in a pastoral or agrarian society which, when it had urban centers, built them in human scale in which family, clan, and tribal ties and mores were powerful protectors of all members. Except for powerful nobility, work was required of all, however arduous or however light it might be; an aged and enfeebled elder could still perform essential work in or near the household.[7]

I'm not suggesting we return to that standard, but I am suggesting there is much physical and spiritual productivity left in those sixty-five and older. Certainly there should never be retirement from God's service. Ministry for Him is a lifelong endeavor. Which is a better—to spend the post-sixty-five years fishing for trout or fishing for men? Upon reaching retirement years, American Christians have opportunity for service unparalleled at any other point in their life. Many have their income requirements met and have freedom to travel without worrying about a daily work grind or young children. Barring poor physical health, this is a great time to do Christian work of some type.

Retirement should never be used as an excuse to pass by on the other side of the road. As long as one has his or her health, this can be a wonderful time to be a good Samaritan to one's fellowman and simultaneously leave a lasting Christian legacy behind. The world will marvel at a man or woman who has worked forty or more years and has a well-deserved retirement coming, yet is using his or her remaining years to help others and to talk about Jesus Christ.

Let me suggest several new perspectives on retirement.

1) Instead of dreaming about retirement as a time when we can play golf or just putter around the house, we should see it as an opportunity for serving the Lord in foreign missions or other compassionate causes.

2) The Lord is allowing us to have a lifetime of training in an occupational talent for a purpose. He wants us to continue to use that skill and training in His service. For example, attorneys can volunteer to assist The Rutherford Institute, The National Legal Foundation, Eagle Forum, Concerned Women for America, and others in their ongoing fight for righteousness. Physicians, dentists, and other professionals can use their skills overseas to help the poor and present the gospel. Almost everyone can volunteer their wisdom and services to help any number of religious or civic organizations that promote morality and the Christian cause.

Intercristo, a nonprofit organization, has a computerized network which can personally match your skills, education, and background with the more than twenty-five thousand current job openings in over twelve hundred Christian organizations in the U.S. and abroad.

Intercristo
19303 Fremont Ave. North
Seattle, WA 98133
(800) 426-1343

3) If our employer allows it, we can take an early retirement so we can begin even sooner to use our mature years for the Lord Jesus Christ. Why remain where we are just to maintain a house or property that will have no enduring value? How much better to use our years of training and experience full-time to build God's Kingdom.

Yes, we should plan for our retirement years, but not in the conventional sense. Rather, let's get serious about ongoing service for Kingdom expansion. Let's not view retirement as waning years in which we grow soft and nonproductive, but rather envision them as exciting years of effectiveness for the Lord Jesus Christ!

Guiding Principle:

Radical Christianity is a lifelong walk in the will of God, and retirement years bring special opportunities we dare not ignore or squander.

REDISCOVER CHRISTIAN RESPECT FOR THE LORD'S DAY

Another area of practical concern which needs reassessment is that of our attitude towards the Lord's day. God in His infinite wisdom knew His people needed one day a week set aside for worship and physical rest. That's why one of the Ten Commandments states, "Remember the Sabbath day by keeping it holy" (Exodus 20:8). It is important to keep this commandment in proper balance so we do not misinterpret its meaning. As we see in the example of the Pharisees in Jesus' day, interpreting this commandment too narrowly creates a legalism which places undue emphasis on externals. Churches which insist you must worship on a particular day of the week are motivated not by internal profit but by external custom and ordinance.

Through Christ, New Testament believers have been set free from Old Testament laws concerning particular customs and times and places of worship (see, for example, Colossians 2:16ff.). Right motivation for obeying commandments about the Lord's day are twofold: 1) the opportunity to participate in public worship, and 2) a bodily need for rest. All else is superfluous.

But, some might object, the Old Testament Sabbath is not synonymous with the New Testament Lord's day. Strictly speaking, this is true, but the principle of one day a week consecrated in a special way to God still stands, and God's people should not take this lightly.

Unfortunately, American culture on the whole displays widespread desecration of the holy day. And sadly, respect for the Lord's Day is waning in Christian circles as well. Many Christians shop on Sundays, eat out on Sundays, and even work on Sundays, as though it were no different from other weekdays.

At the same time, Sunday is to be a day of rest, not a day of idleness. Sunday should be a day busily spent serving God and ministering to family and personal needs. That is impossible to do if we devote the day to televised football, yard mowing, car repairs, or extensive housework. Sunday should be a *special* day, a *holy* day set apart for God's Word and for rest. Somewhere along the way we have confused our freedom as Christians with license to use the day any way we please. Routine Sunday shopping, for example, shows a frivolous disregard for the Lord's day. Eating out or shopping on Sundays (unless absolutely necessary) may do the same. It's time for radical Christians to protest business as usual on Sundays in a way that communicates the true purpose for the Lord's day and their love for Him.

The key to understanding this radical Christian principle lies not in legalistic observance, but in the word "sanctify," which means "to keep holy among us." The crucial question for each of us is, How can I observe the Lord's day as holy in my life?

The first and most obvious way to keep the Lord's day holy is to *occupy ourselves with God's Word and its teachings*. This means being faithful in attendance at church and Sunday school because we want to, from the heart, not just from force of habit. This means being ready beforehand for worship. Staying up late the night before to watch the Saturday late show or a favorite video betrays good preparation for church and allows Satan to make us stumble. The same thing can be said for Sunday afternoons. To flip on the television set the minute you arrive home from church and watch football all Sunday afternoon doesn't show good stewardship on the special day of worship.

A second way to keep the Lord's day holy is to *cease from routine secular activities*. God asks that we turn aside from our ordinary activities one day in seven. That's not too much to ask, especially since it's for our good and His glory. Many Christians honor the Lord's day by refraining from personal work, but then make others work by eating out or going grocery shopping. This is an apparent inconsistency radical Christians should seek to avoid—again, not out of compulsion, but willingly and out of love for God.

Insofar as it is reasonable and possible, radical Christians seek jobs that will not require work on Sundays. Occasionally Sunday hours may be necessary, though efforts should be made to avoid employment that routinely requires one to forfeit public worship. Even in occupations that perform works of necessity, such as hospitals, police, fire fighters, public utilities, the military, etc., the employer will often, upon request, rotate shifts in respect for one's religious commitment.

No nation that disregards the Lord's day has ever prospered long. Adam brought marriage and the Sabbath with him out of the Garden, and neither can be disregarded without paying a price. When the children of Israel went into the Promised Land, God told them to let their land rest every seven years, and He would give them as much in six years as in seven. For 490 years (seventy seventh years) they disregarded that law. Then Nebuchadnezzar took them captive into Babylon, where they spent seventy years in captivity; thus the land regained its seventy sabbaths of rests. We can give God His day or He will take it from us. God honors those who honor Him (cf. Isaiah 58:13, 14). Greedy merchandisers will always chafe under the commandment to sanctify God's day, but we should neither be party to their ways nor contribute to their profits on the Lord's day.

After spending millions of dollars in efficiency studies, corporate industry has concluded that you can productively squeeze just so many hours out of a man. Without proper rest a man starts to lose his drive and energy, and his efforts become counterproductive. It is no wonder Christ recognized the Sabbath benefits for man (Matthew 12:1-8; Mark 3:1-6). Though I do not agree with the legalistic Sabbath requirement of certain Saturday worshipers, I do admire their commitment to a day dedicated to worship and kept free of toil and trade, their keeping a primary focus on God. If only the whole Christian community would give God's day such priority!

Guiding Principle:
Radical Christians are eager to honor a day which gives preeminence to worship, spiritual growth, physical rest, and the mutual uplifting of family members.

ENCOURAGE A HEALTHY INTEREST IN READING

What does reading have to do with radical Christianity? The bridge is built of priorities and values. In our high-tech, thrill-seeking, visually-oriented society, encouraging children to read for pleasure is indeed radical. Most of our society's modern diversions profit little when it comes to personal growth. A large proportion of video games, for example, are non-educational and non-productive. Teens and adults can get so addicted to TV or movies, whether at the theater or on their VCR, that they tune out their families and friends. Those who spend their recreational hours reading a good book tap into a vast storehouse of both divine wisdom and collective human knowledge. The best way for adults to teach this to their children is to read to them when they are small. Instead of huddling around the television, let's show our children the pleasure and value of getting into a good book.

Children need to be *encouraged* to read because it won't happen naturally. Compliment them when they set and meet a reading goal. (Reading one book every week or two is a healthy target.) Provide ample opportunities for reading. In addition to our personal book collections at home, we and our children should make regular trips to the public library. Through constant exposure and encouragement, children develop a love for reading. One Christian book club many children enjoy is:

God's Word Publications
P.O. Box 2330
Asheville, NC 28802-2330
(704) 253-8063

Radical Christians screen all reading material being received by family members. Gossip tabloids have no place in the Christian home. We must be on the alert for any form of pornography in popular magazines, even some of the best ones. We need to reexamine the value of any magazine or catalog that promotes lust or leads the mind to think impurely, whether overtly or not. Some Christians subscribe to certain magazines to see how the other side is thinking. There is nothing wrong in that per se. However, we must be aware that many popular weekly news magazines are saturated with suggestive advertising, not to mention unwholesome or morally biased articles which reflect anti-Christian values.

Good reading material is opened with expectation and closed with profit. The selection of all reading material ought to be guided by the following Scripture: "'Everything is permissible'—but not everything is beneficial. 'Everything is permissible'—but not everything is constructive" (1 Corinthians 10:23). Before we subscribe to a magazine, we must ask ourselves, Is it beneficial? Is it constructive? Does it promote impure thinking? The answers to these questions will help us allow only valuable reading material into our homes.

Guiding Principle:

Does that particular book or magazine we are interested in edify? Can our families read it without being subjected to suggestive advertising? Does it contain material that could cause family members to stumble or will numb their sensitivity to righteousness?

It is prudent to guard our hearts, even in regard to our reading material. What we read should be as edifying as it is informative. There is much good, wholesome, and informative reading available. The following are some suggested newspapers and magazines for various subjects and age levels:

For National and World News

Human Events
150 East 35th Street
New York, NY 10157

National Review
422 1st Street S.E.
Washington, DC 20003

The Capital Report
122 C Street N.W.
Washington, DC 20001

Conservative Digest
National Press Building
Suite 1210
Washington, DC 20045
(202) 622-8919

New Dimensions
P.O. Box 811
Grants Pass, OR 97526
(800) 866-9499

FOR LIGHT READING ENJOYMENT

Readers Digest
Pleasantville, NY 10570

Moody Monthly
820 N. LaSalle Street
Chicago, IL 60610

Saturday Evening Post
1100 Waterway Blvd.
Indianapolis, IN 46202

FOR SPIRITUAL ENCOURAGEMENT

Discipleship Journal
Box 6000
Colorado Springs, CO 80934

Focus on the Family
801 Corporate Center
Pomona, CA 91799

Mountain Movers
1445 Boonville
Springfield, MO 65802

FOR UPDATES ON CURRENT EVENTS AFFECTING THE FAMILY

Family in America
934 N. Main
Rockford, IL 61103

Citizen
Focus On the Family
801 Corporate Center
Pomona, CA 91799

Phyllis Schlafly Report
Box 618
Alton, IL 62002

Magazines for Children

Clubhouse Magazine
Focus on the Family
801 Corporate Center
Pomona, CA 91799

God's World Today
Box 2330
Asheville, NC 28802-2330
(somewhat of a Christian *Weekly Reader* for grades K-12)

In addition to reading, children enjoy listening to stories and music on cassette. My children listen to praise and Bible-story tapes almost every evening before going to sleep. Stories on tape help children use their imagination to re-create instructive events and experience growing faith. One source for these is:

Dramatized Bible Cassettes
(with Uncle Dan & Aunt Sue)
Available through Family Life Institute
P.O. Box 234
Nordland, WA 98658

Available on cassette from this organization are Old Testament stories (forty C-45 cassettes), *Life of Jesus* series (twenty C-45 cassettes), *Paul and the Apostles* (fifteen C-45 cassettes), and *Adventures in Life* series (character-building tapes). I highly recommend them all! Great music tapes are also available.

Other cassette manufacturers offering wholesome children's music include:

Word Kids' Music Club
P.O. Box 10804
Des Moines, IA 50380-0804

Kids' Praise
Maranatha Music
P.O. Box 31050
Laguna Hills, CA 92654-1050

Wee Sing Silly Songs
Price/Stern/Sloan Publishers, Inc.
410 N. La Cienega Blvd.
Los Angeles, CA 90048

Hosanna Kids' Praise
P.O. Box Z
Mobile, AL 36616

NINE

Radical Christian Living, Part IV

*L*et's continue our practical discussion of how our families can be truly Christian in our post-Christian age.

RECAPTURE A MENTALITY OF MENTORING

Radical Christians are eager to restore another lost art—mentoring. In years gone by, this was the chief method of learning. Agrarian fathers mentored their sons; mothers mentored their daughters. In this way parents taught masculinity and femininity in their proper forms, what work was and how to carry it out, the essence of character, the formation of values, the various responsibilities to be fulfilled in home, church and society.

By contrast, mentoring today is near extinction. It has been virtually lost in the home, since most children are separated from their parents for the better part of the day and garner an average of only eight to eleven minutes of their parents' time daily. It is lost in educational circles also, since faculty and students scarcely meet outside the classroom. It is lost in the church, where one-on-one discipleship has been overshadowed by television ministries, sundry evangelistic programs, musical and theatrical outreach productions, and pulpit evangelism.

Mentoring must be rediscovered if we are to redevelop maturity and character depth in our families and churches—in our society.

Virtually all training of Bible personalities was accomplished in such a context. Moses mentored Joshua, Naomi Ruth, Elijah Elisha, Jesus the twelve, Barnabas Paul, Paul Timothy, and Priscilla and Aquila Apollos. Today we desperately need godly men and women who are willing to mentor others, starting with their own family and widening the circle from there.

Mentors teach primarily by example and close supervision. They offer much-needed individualized assistance in areas such as character, encouragement, discipline/correction, confrontation, and accountability. The goal is to develop the other person's maximum potential for Jesus Christ in every aspect of his or her life, with special emphasis on evangelism and discipleship. A Christian mentor not only teaches his or her protégé how to read the Bible, pray, witness, worship God, and live in obedience, but models Christian conduct and character for him or her until that person becomes an effective discipler himself or herself. This is the ultimate goal of all discipleship.

The chart below shows the rate of people won to Christ by new believers with no discipling compared to those who receive disciplined training. Note the substantial conversion rate difference between the two.

One Convert Per Week: No Training	Years	One Convert Per Year: Trained
53	1	2
105	2	4
157	3	8
209	4	16
261	5	32
313	6	64
365	7	128
417	8	256
469	9	512
521	10	1024
573	11	2048
625	12	4096
1613	32	4,294,967,296
1665	33	8,589,934,592

The column on the left assumes that a Christian will win *one person to Christ each week* without any ongoing discipleship training. In thirty-three years he will have led 1,665 people to Christ. The column on the right assumes that a Christian will win *one person to Christ each year*, but also disciples that person into Christian maturity. In thirty-three short years, the same number of years our Lord walked on the earth, they will have reached 8,589,934,592 people for Christ, a figure which far exceeds the current population of the world.

Jesus, our model, intensely discipled the twelve. Though He did what He could to help the multitudes, He devoted Himself primarily to those twelve, in order that masses could be saved. His evangelism strategy involved training dedicated men who would carry on His work when He was gone. And as the ministry of Christ lengthened into the second and third years, He gave increasingly more time to the disciples, not less. When He departed this world He had actually spent more time with His disciples than with everybody else in the world put together.[1] Hence, discipleship was not only personally practiced by Jesus, but remains His sole plan for bringing a lost world back to Him.

There are two books about discipleship which every radical Christian should read: Robert E. Coleman's *The Master Plan of Evangelism* and Dr. Ted W. Engstrom's *The Fine Art of Mentoring*. Taken together, these two books lay out the strategy and method of effectively mentoring others.

Part of the problem with the church today is that we have too much individualism and not enough accountability. A large percentage of pastors and Christian workers have never been discipled. Some see no reason to maintain such a relationship with someone more spiritually mature than themselves. Even church leaders have fallen into sin because they had no one to whom they were accountable. Whatever the reason—pride, ignorance, shortage of mentors—this practice of being a spiritual lone wolf has filtered down to the pew. God desires His body to be interactive and mutually accountable. He wants genuine mentoring—discipleship—to take place.[2] Only in this way can we hope to alleviate the pitfalls of self-accountability.

Mentoring is one of the best and most proven methods for building a strong family, church, and society. James Dobson, Charles Swindoll, Bruce Larson, Tony Campolo, Charles Colson, and Ted Engstrom have all been mentored. If we have not been discipled, we should seek out a mature Christian who will serve as our mentor. If we have had the privilege of being discipled, we can now experience the joy of passing on to others what we have learned.

Guiding Principle:

In following the Lord Jesus Christ, we must be alert for opportunities to lead others into an increasing knowledge of God, to disciple them to the glory of God.

MASTER THE MODERN MUSIC MORASS

As Christian parents we must face the fact that modern rock can have a detrimental effect on our children. Since the nature of such music seems self-apparent, I won't spend much time on this issue, but I do want to underscore its dangers. Numerous police investigations have suggested a strong connection between heavy metal rock and teenage activities ranging from violent behavior to suicide. A high percentage of heavy metal rock lyrics extol such evil behavior as rape, incest, homosexuality, sadomasochism, and bestiality. Modern secular music also glamorizes drug and alcohol use, glorifies death and violent rebellion, and promotes hatred of parents, teachers, and other authority figures. Even the names of some groups are revealing (for example, Venom, Slayer, Poison, Motley Crue, Grateful Dead). So are some album titles, such as "Hell Awaits," "Dirty Mind," and "I Want Your Sex," one of George Michael's best selling hits.

The lyrics of much heavy metal rock should especially horrify Christians. Consider the message of Venom, whose message was clearly stated on the album jacket:

> We're possessed by all that's evil;
> The death of your God we demand.
> We spit at the virgin you worship,
> And sit at Lord Satan's left hand.

A song by Prince entitled "Sister" unleashed these words on young listeners:

> My sister never made love to anyone but me.
> Incest is everything it's said to be.

Some Christian teenagers tell their parents, "I don't listen to the words . . . I just like the beat." But youngsters pick up more content than they realize. Furthermore, researchers Harvey Bird of Fairleigh Dickinson University in Rutherford, New Jersey, and Gervasia Schreckenberg of Georgian Court College in Lakewood, New Jersey, have discovered that even the beat of modern rock is cause for concern. Experiments have shown that rats exposed to rock music for eight weeks take much longer to find their way through an ordinary maze. When dissected, their brains reveal abnormal neuron structures in the region associated with learning and memory.[3] Christians can in no way support the rock music industry as a whole.

Also, we must not think it is harmless if our children plaster posters of rock stars on their bedroom walls. Children are natural hero-worshipers. Sustained poster imagery encourages them to see rock stars as idols and to pick up pop rock values, many of which are antithetical to radical Christianity.

Returning to the matter of music lyrics, psychiatrist Robert S. Demski, chief of staff at Laurel Ridge Hospital in San Antonio, says, "Once something is learned at an early age, it may be difficult to unlearn."[4] Christian parents must give direction and leadership in the area of music. We must not allow our beloved sons and daughters to brand their minds with filth and debauchery by hearing music with evil lyrics. The common slogan encouraged to reject drug use is appropriate here as well: "Just say no! I don't want to hear it!"

Further, we must tell our children *why* heavy metal music is unwholesome. We must teach them the importance of discernment regarding the music to which they listen. We must pray with them about these matters and encourage an interest in wholesome music, including Christian music (praise tapes are great!) and the classics.

Guiding Principle:

As parents and as committed Christians, we must reject any music which has anti-Christian content and must teach our sons and daughters to do the same. We must not only tell our children what music is wrong but why.

CHOOSE SANCTIFIED CHRISTIANITY OVER LEGALISM

There is a great difference between a Biblical approach to family living and a legalistic one. Legalism is a blending of justification and sanctification. One Biblical heresy of this type, called "infused grace," teaches that our salvation depends in part upon the good works we produce. Such a view implies we can contribute in some way to our salvation, which Scripture clearly states is impossible (cf. Romans 3:28; 4:5; Galatians 2:16; Ephesians 2:8, 9; Philippians 3:9). The Holy Scriptures are clear: we are saved by grace alone (*sola gratia*), through faith (*sola fide*), apart from works of the law.

Personal holiness—good works—in no way creates or preserves saving faith. True believers look continually and exclusively to the merits of a sinless Christ who secured salvation by His substitutionary atonement and victorious resurrection from the dead.

While we cannot put sanctification before justification, there is an inseparable connection between the two. Faith alone saves, but it rightly and properly should be followed by sanctified living. In fact, where there is no sanctification there is no faith (James 2:14-26). Furthermore, while personal holiness does not create saving faith, an evil and unpleasing lifestyle will in some ways destroy faith (cf. 1 Timothy 1:18-20; 2 Timothy 2:16-18).

Radical Christians seek personal holiness for four reasons. First, *it shows love for God and demonstrates a longing to please Him* (Hebrews 13:16). A husband may occasionally bring his wife some flowers, not out of compulsion, but because he wants to show his love and devotion. How much greater a privilege it is to show our love for God. It should be our fervent desire to lead our families in serving God rather than Satan and sin. Indeed, we have been redeemed for this very purpose (Romans 6:1-23; Ephesians 2:10; Titus 2:12-14).

Second, *holiness is an external testimony to the world that we are disciples of the Lord Jesus Christ* (1 John 3:7, 10). External newness of life bears witness that we have experienced internal spiritual transformation.

Third, *holiness demonstrates the truth of the gospel to an unsaved world, creating in unbelievers a desire to hear the saving message of Christ* (Matthew 5:13-16; 1 Peter 2:12; 3:1, 2). They see in us a power greater than ourselves, for "we have this treasure in jars of clay to show that this all-surpassing power is from God and not from us" (2 Corinthians 4:7).

Fourth, *our striving for holiness encourages and comforts our fellow brothers and sisters in Christ* (2 Corinthians 1:5-7).

While personal holiness has this fourfold aim, we must continually keep in mind that the Christian life in its entirety is produced and energized only by the work of Christ. The obvious conclusion of all this is that seeking a radical Christian life of personal holiness and separation is not legalism. Rather, it is the outworking of the power of God in Christians' lives. As the Apostle Paul wrote:

> I urge you, brothers, in view of God's mercy, to offer your bodies as living sacrifices, holy and pleasing to God—which is your spiritual worship. Do not conform any longer to the pattern of this

world, but be transformed by the renewing of your mind. (Romans 12:1, 2)

Guiding Principle:

Radical Christians do not try to maintain a religious routine but rather allow God to reproduce the character of Christ in and through them day by day.

FIGHT THE GOOD FIGHT FOR FAMILY HOLINESS

Godly family life is admittedly not easy in our wicked and perverse generation. The struggle of the spirit against the flesh is difficult. *Flourishing families take radical steps to guard their hearts and their minds.* Believers are admonished to "continue to work out your salvation with fear and trembling" (Philippians 2:12). This passage has puzzled some Christians. Here is the best explanation of this verse that I've come across:

> This is the same fear and trembling as that mentioned in Eph. 6:5. Joseph exhibited it when Potiphar's wife tempted him, and he exclaimed, "How can I do this great wickedness, and sin against God?" This holy fear trembles at the thought of doing or omitting anything that will offend God, compel him to turn away, and thus endanger our salvation. It is not a dread that we may after all be damned; *it is shrinking from all carelessness in faith and in life.* The Christian does not dread God who gives him the life-giving gospel (v. 16, "life's Word"), but he *dreads the poison of sin that robs him of strength to work out the salvation of himself.* So far from killing the Christian's joy in the Lord, this fear increases his joy by increasing his assurance that the Lord is with him for his salvation.[5] (emphasis mine)

Each and every day we enter into spiritual warfare. Only compromisers do not face the intensity of this struggle. The fight is relentless and offers no respite in this life, for there is continual tension between our old and new natures. Using his own life as a chalkboard, Paul describes this perpetual struggle:

> For I have the desire to do what is good, but I cannot carry it out. For what I do is not the good I want to do; no, the evil I do not want to do—this I keep on doing. Now if I do what I do not want to do, it is no longer I who do it, but it is sin living in me that does it. So I find this law at work: When I want to do good, evil is right there with me. For in my inner being I delight in God's law; but I see another law at work in the members of my body, waging war against the law of my mind and making me a prisoner of the law of sin at work within my members. (Romans 7:18-23)

Families seeking to serve God wholeheartedly will find the struggle no easier. We may know the Bible backwards and forwards; we may be Spirit-filled Christians; we may walk out of a revival service and feel like we have the world by the tail. But we must still continually battle our old nature, which constantly raises its ugly head to try to force us into compromise or defeat.

Winning a victory once in a while is not enough. The battle to keep our families godly constantly rages on. Gideon is an example of one who failed to avoid spiritual warfare. In his early life he magnificently led the people with his God-fearing, heroic actions; but later in life he fell into deplorable self-indulgence. His compromise pulled down his family and in fact the whole nation (Judges 8:24-27). Apparently it was easier for Gideon to honor God in a courageous act during a national emergency than in everyday life. The latter requires a different and sometimes a greater kind of courage.

The Bible tells of many men who began well (Lot, Samson, Solomon) but were sidetracked from maintaining a life consecrated to God—and each paid a high price. We never arrive at a point in this life where we can throw caution and battle readiness to the wind. Perhaps this is what Paul meant when he said, "if you think you are standing firm, be careful that you don't fall!" (1 Corinthians 10:12). Peter gives a similar warning: "be on your guard so that you may not be carried away by the error of lawless men and fall from your secure position" (2 Peter 3:17).

Guiding Principle:
Serious Christians do not underestimate the importance of spiritual warfare in their homes, but rather fight the good fight, relying on the power, love, and wisdom of God.

ESTABLISH EFFECTIVE DEFENSE MECHANISMS

Serious Christians must continually defend their hearts against all forms of temptation (Matthew 26:41—"watch and pray"). To "watch" not only means to look out for temptation, but also to take extraordinary steps to protect our moral and spiritual purity. Temptation comes from three sources—the world, the flesh, and the Devil. We must guard our family life daily and gain victory over all three.

Temptations from *the world* are relentless and powerful. The worldly maladies we examined in Chapters 1 and 2 comprise insidious cultural attacks on the Christian family. To gain the victory we must limit our exposure to the world's allurements. For example, some Christians need to eliminate all morally compromising entertainment from their lifestyle. Others need to cancel subscriptions to certain publications which have articles or advertisements that routinely appeal to unhealthy sexual appetites. Some need to examine their children's classrooms or the role models they are exhibiting as dads or moms. For others, the western practice of dating needs to be replaced with more constructive social patterns.

Our sinful *flesh* also tempts us (James 1:14). This is why the New

Testament uses strong phrases such as "mortify," "crucify," and "cut off" to tell us how to treat the flesh. Shocked by the wickedness in man, Jeremiah said, "The heart is deceitful above all things and beyond cure. Who can understand it?" (Jeremiah 17:9). The Apostle Paul, coming to grips with his own sinful tendencies, cried out, "What a wretched man I am!" (Romans 7:24). The battle is not easy for any of us.

We must accept the truth: evil lurks in our own hearts, and this inner evil is constantly seeking outward expression. We struggle continually with our sinful flesh and must use God-given physical, emotional and spiritual safeguards to protect ourselves in all areas where we are vulnerable. Our flesh has a proneness toward idolatry, lust, wastefulness of time, manipulation or criticism of others, the accumulation of unnecessary material possessions, and literally hundreds of other wicked tendencies. We gain victory over our flesh when we stand guard against inner temptations and seek divine assistance in making honest self-examination and living holy lives.

There are also temptations that come from *the Devil* himself. Peter warns us that a fiendishly busy enemy is constantly seeking ways to bring our families to ruin (1 Peter 5:8). This evil one is described as "the prince of this world" (John 12:31). He does not work alone (Matthew 25:41), but has many fallen angels as devilish cohorts (cf. Mark 5:9). Not only is he powerful, he is deceitful as well: "Satan himself masquerades as an angel of light" (2 Corinthians 11:14). He knows how to quote, misquote, and twist Scripture and to use the church and compromising leaders for his own ends if they stray from the Lord's path (Genesis 3:1-6; Matthew 4:6).

One of the key tasks for family leadership is to build strong defenses—a Christian Strategic Defense Initiative. Wise Solomon said, "The prudent see danger and take refuge, but the simple keep going and suffer for it" (Proverbs 27:12). A family that flourishes in this life must be on constant patrol, watching for any and all moral and spiritual danger. The Christian family must set up necessary precautions to protect vulnerable areas in both family and personal life.

The radical Christian family goes out of its way to keep its focus on God and to maintain separation from the world. This doesn't come easily. Holy living is rugged and demanding; it exacts a price. Daily we must battle in the trenches of a sinful world, being thankful for every opportunity to serve God. We need to enact safeguards and disciplines that others may dub unnecessary, overreactive or legalistic (1 Thessalonians 5:22). We may have to bear criticism, mockery and scorn for our commitment to God's standards. Sometimes this criticism even comes from those within the church. Sometimes it comes from relatives. This all hurts terribly! But we understand and expect it, for this is the cost of discipleship.

Guiding Principle:
The Christian family which truly follows Christ is ever on guard against temptation and moral compromise. This ought never to be taken lightly!

We have examined ten practical areas where Christian families can make a difference in personal life and in the world. The suggestions are simple yet radical considering the humanistic culture we live in. Applying practical steps of Christian living may not make us rich and famous, but they will help our families flourish as God meant them to do.

TEN

What? My Family Missionaries?

The discussion of radical Christianity must include what it means to be light in a dark world, and being light of necessity includes personal involvement in evangelism and missions. Families flourish when they get in tune with their divine purpose, and God's foremost eternal plan for mankind is that people come to a saving knowledge of and personal relationship with Jesus Christ. We have already looked at numerous areas which set Christian families apart—families that want to make an impact for Jesus Christ. Nothing demonstrates fiery devotion to Jesus Christ like personal commitment to the fulfillment of the Great Commission He gave us. This is the work for which Christ entered the world and for which He gave His life. Christian families are a very important part of God's strategy for evangelization in our nation and around the world.

If Christianity maintains its current global conversion rate, we will not keep pace with the growth of world population. Thus greater personal commitment and sacrifice are called for. In fact, without a trend reversal Christian evangelization efforts actually threaten to move backwards. (A chart in Appendix A, "Population Growth from 1934 to 1984," shows the comparative growth of Christianity in relation to other religions over a fifty-year period. Another chart, "Islam Exceeds Christians by Year 2100," shows that population growth among Muslims is increasing faster than among Christians.) We can't blame any of this on God, for His mercy and grace are never restrained. But we can blame the church, as long as we remember who the church is. *We* are the church. Families are a significant component in the church. In fact, the family is somewhat of a microcosm of the church, the father being the family pastor.

ARE WE HOARDING THE GOSPEL?

Western Christianity is ineffective in world outreach primarily because of individual selfishness and indifference. Too many think of themselves as American Christians instead of World Christians. Consider this:

> Only 9 percent of the world's population speaks English, and yet 94 percent of *all ordained preachers* in the whole world minister to the 9 percent who speak English. And 96 percent of *all* Christian finances are spent in the United States on 6 percent of the world's population. Only 4 percent of all Christian money is spent on missionary efforts to reach the other 94 percent of the world's population!"[1]

There are are over one million full-time Christian workers in the United States, while half of the world's population have approximately 2,500 full-time Christian workers. Yes, we ought to witness to those we can here at home, but there is a drastic shortage of spiritual laborers in other lands. We must not hoard the gospel. Christian families in America are at a crossroads. They can either choose a life of militant mission-mindedness and personal soul-winning, or they can remain under the selfish wings of introverted, indifferent, mother-hen Christianity.

HOW LOST IS MANKIND?

Tacit universalism has wormed its way into the mind-set of modern American Christians. This is obvious by the lack of widespread personal urgency in the believing community towards evangelization in America and around the world. The notion that somehow all people will be eternally O.K. (whatever that means) has insidiously infiltrated the Christian church and must be resisted.

We dare not forget that the Bible nowhere describes Hell as an overnight experience or a spiritual hand-slapping! Instead, it describes it as everlasting punishment, unending agony and misery, incomprehensible soul-torture, and eternal condemnation.[2] It is a place of "weeping and gnashing of teeth" where one's "worm does not die, and the fire is not quenched" (Matthew 8:12; Mark 9:48). In Hell there will be no furloughs or second chances, but rather utter separation from God without the slightest hope of any divine mercy or comfort. Yet, lurking in the minds of many Christians is the idea that somehow unbelievers will at the last minute be pardoned or at least spared from the ultimate horrors of Hell. Such thinking is un-Biblical and un-Christian. Worse, it undercuts the imperative of gospel proclamation by the Christian community.

Some appease their conscience with the thought, "At least *I'm* saved," as though it doesn't really matter what happens to others. *We need to reaffirm the Biblical truth of the lostness of man.* Unless the guilt of sin is removed by faith in Christ, man will indeed suffer eternal death, which is not just the cessation of man's existence, but eternal and perpetual torment. Only trust in the atoning work accomplished through the blood of Jesus Christ provides life for those who are dead in their sins. Without saving faith a man is as without hope as a skydiver without a parachute. But to go beyond this analogy, at physical death the torment just begins. "It is a dreadful thing to fall into the hands of the living God" (Hebrews 10:31). Without saving faith all human beings face eternal damnation in hideous and inexplicable agony of both body and soul. We must face the truth—"He that believeth not shall be damned" (Mark 16:16, KJV).

The lostness of unregenerate man is an unalterable reality. People the world over desperately need a substantial and effective Christian witness. But before that will happen we must be constrained by the love of Christ to develop a burden and a compassion for lost souls. Soul-winning and discipleship are to be all-pervading concerns in the radical Christian family.

A MATTER OF LIFE AND DEATH

We need to fully understand and accept the imperative of the Christian mission. Chiseled into the cornerstone of every Christian church should be these words: Personal involvement in evangelism/missions is not just an *urgency*, but an *emergency*. George Peters offers this lucid observation:

> We are all acquainted with emergency situations. Emergency landings by aircraft are familiar announcements. An emergency means either a landing or a crash with all its horror and tragedy. Emergencies come upon us uninvited and challenge our strength and genius. They involve crisis of life and death. When the siren breaks into the stillness of night, when flames burst from roof and windows, when firemen feverishly raise their ladders and race up into the smoke and flames, risking their own welfare and lives in order to rescue calling voices, we are aware that an emergency exists which taxes men to the utmost. Emergencies are crisis experiences.
>
> No emergency, however, can compare with the emergency of gospel proclamation. Here we face a crisis not only of death and life but of spiritual and eternal welfare or eternal separation, destitution and death. Here, indeed, is an emergency. We need to think soberly, to realize, at least in part, the emergency into which the presence and possession of the gospel has placed us. It is an emergency of infinite significance involving the eternal bliss or misery of countless multitudes.[3]

There is an emergency manpower shortage of soul-winners! Such ought to be the words of every commencement speaker at every Christian school, Bible college, and seminary across the country. It should also be the words every Christian father and mother pass on to their children. The great C. H. Spurgeon described this desperate crisis in these words:

> The vessel is wrecked, the sailors are perishing; they are clinging to the rigging as best they can; they are being washed off one by one! Good God, they die before our eyes, and yet there is the lifeboat stanch and trim. We want men! Men to man the boat! Here are the oars, but never an arm to use them! What is to be done? Here is the gallant boat, able to leap from billow to billow, only men are wanted! Are there none?[4]

In 1883 Joseph Barnby, a Congregational pastor in Philadelphia, with the words of Isaiah 6:8 in mind, was inspired to write a beautiful hymn:

> Hark! the voice of Jesus crying,
> "Who will go and work today?
> Fields are white and harvest waiting,
> Who will bear the sheaves away?"
> Loud and long the Master calleth,
> Rich reward He offers thee;
> Who will answer, gladly saying,
> "Here am I, send me, send me"?
>
> Let none hear you idly saying,
> "There is nothing I can do,"
> While the souls of men are dying
> And the Master calls for you.
> Take the task He gives you gladly,
> Let His work your pleasure be;
> Answer quickly when He calleth,
> "Here am I, send me, send me!"[5]

The facts speak for themselves. Over 2.2 billion individuals in 12,000 people groups have never had the opportunity to hear the

gospel of Jesus Christ. These numbers don't even include an additional 1.3 billion others who are in so-called "reached" groups where there is some Christian presence. These too need to be evangelized. The harvest field includes (from *The Go Manual*):
- Many million Muslims in 4,000 unreached people groups.
- 550 million Hindus in 2,000 unreached people groups.
- 275 million Buddhists in 1,000 unreached people groups.
- 150 million Han Chinese in 1,000 unreached people groups.
- 140 million tribal peoples in 3,000 unreached people groups.
- 225 million people in 1,000 assorted other unreached people groups in North America, Africa, Asia and other western nations.

The Biblical mandate has been muddied in many corners of the church. We must face the truth: people without saving faith in Christ are lost and must be found. Jesus shows the ends to which we must go to find the lost in His Parable of the Lost Sheep: "Suppose one of you has a hundred sheep and loses one of them. *Does he not leave the ninety-nine in the open country and go after the lost sheep until he finds it?* . . . there is more rejoicing in heaven over one sinner who repents than over ninety-nine righteous persons who do not need to repent" (Luke 15:4, 7). Implicit in this parable is God's overriding concern for the redemption of the eternally lost. While God will not abandon the sheep already in His fold, *He clearly wants the lost sheep found.* There is nothing more spiritual and God-pleasing than reconciling the lost to God.

Donald McGavran describes the confusion in today's Christian community:

> At base, the trouble is that mere search, detached witness—without the deep wish to convert, without wholehearted persuasion, and with what amounts to a fear of the numerical increase of Christians—is not Biblically justified. *Mere search is not what God wants. God wants His lost children found.*
>
> . . . any formula which limits the Christian to search or to neutralist witness, whether out of respect for the sovereignty of God or fear of practicing religious imperialism, has an artificial ring to

it. It fits a system, not the New Testament. In avoiding the manipulation of persons, it falls into the sin of passing by on the other side. It may enable Christians to continue witness to an unresponsive society, but that does not make the formula pleasing to God or true to the New Testament Church.[6]

We must seek and find!

Guiding Principle:

Effective world evangelization depends on families accepting a responsible role in winning the lost. Flourishing families will rediscover their place and purpose in the mission of God.

MUST WE REALLY "GO"?

The clear command of Christ in Matthew 28:19 is "Go," not "stay"! Inviting unsaved American friends to your church has its place. Passing out tracts as God leads can result in people won to Christ. Witnessing for Christ on the home front is important. But we must also recognize the overwhelming, greater need in other lands around the world. Gospel-saturated Americans have one Christian worker for every 230 people, while those who have never heard the gospel have less than one worker for every 450,000 souls.[7] While many nations have little credible Christian witness, every Sunday more than eighty-five million Americans are in church, and 125 million are taking in Christian radio and television programs regularly.[8]

Though most Americans are not Christians, few can claim ignorance of the gospel. There are roughly 340,000 churches in the United States. The spiritual affluence of the West is also evident in the sheer number of Christian radio stations, television stations and cable networks, and bookstores. There are hundreds of Christian magazines. There are more than ample spiritual resources in the United States to meet the needs of our 250 million people. The heathen in the United States are heathen by choice, while the unconverted multitudes in Third-World nations are heathen because they haven't heard the Good News.

God is a God of outreach, and He commands us all to take part in personal evangelism. We must each, individually and as families, seek His guidance in where and how He wants us to share the gospel. Personal and family involvement in missions is the hallmark of true Christianity. Commenting on this thought James Stewart says:

> The fact is, belief in missions and belief in Christ stand and fall together. To say "I believe that God so loved the world, that in Christ He gave everything He had, gave His very self," to use such words not lightly or conventionally but in spirit and in truth, means that the one who uses them binds himself irrevocably to make self-giving the controlling principle of life; and this is the very essence of missions. To put it otherwise, the concern for world evangelization is not something tacked on to a man's personal Christianity, which he may take or leave as he chooses; it is rooted indefeasibly in the character of the God who has come to us in Christ Jesus. Thus it can never be the province of a few enthusiasts, a sideline or a speciality of those who happen to have a bent that way. It is the distinctive mark of being a Christian. To accept Christ is to enlist under a missionary banner. It is quite impossible to be (in the Pauline phrase) "in Christ" and not participate in Christ's mission in the world. In fact, here is the surest test whether we have truly grasped what Christ was doing by His life and death and resurrection, or whether we have failed even to begin to understand the gospel that He brought.[9]

SOUL-WINNING AND BIBLICAL CHRISTIANITY

The imperative of evangelizing a lost world is the clear mission of Biblical Christianity. Biblical Christianity and soul-winning are unavoidably interrelated. This is no surprise, for winning the lost was the very heartbeat of our Lord's life. He declared His life's mission to be to "seek and to save what was lost" (Luke 19:10). His redeeming work gave us an example to follow. His post-resurrection command gave us a mission to fulfill. And on Pentecost, the birthday of the church, the Holy Spirit's power was poured out for global evangelization. Should we not look back to the dawn of Christianity and vow to emulate those early believers who stormed the world for Christ with their Spirit-inspired, evangelistic zeal?

Fired by the "power" of the Holy Ghost (Greek *dunamis,* from which we get the word dynamite), Paul had a burning desire "to preach the gospel where Christ was not known" (Romans 15:20). We need to put a little of that dynamite under our church pews today! Everywhere he went, Paul preached Christ and led people to the Lord. Each New Testament book Paul wrote came out of the needs of young churches filled with new converts.

The early church took the Great Commission to heart. In a little over thirty-three and a half years first-century Christians evangelized the whole then-known world. Filled with a sense of gratitude, responsibility, and concern for the lost, the early church lived and breathed evangelism. Beyond all doubt soul-winning was the distinguishing mark of early Christianity.

To this day, effective witnessing remains at the top of the Lord's priority list for every one of His followers. It is the watershed between the spiritually ardent and the spiritually indifferent. A survey by Campus Crusade for Christ revealed that 98 percent of church members are not regularly sharing their faith in Christ.[10] How can we be light to a dark world unless this lethargy is changed to fervency?

Christian families can help bring about a spiritual resurgence of soul-winning by restructuring their personal priorities and life goals. The Soviets want to restructure their dead economy, but have little money or power to bring it about. American Christians have the vast resources of God, including the awesome power of the Holy Spirit, available to them. Through local church sponsorship or by working with evangelistic para-church organizations, Christian families can help restore the fires of soul-winning to American Christianity.

EXCUSES THAT WILL NOT WASH

There are several common rationalizations American Christians use to exempt themselves from missionary or evangelistic responsibility. When we take a good look at these excuses, we see how unacceptable they really are.

Excuse #1: "Mission Work Is Only for Full-time Missionaries or Christian Workers"

Not so! At its inception Christianity was a lay movement, and it continued in that capacity for quite some time. The apostles inevitably became the "professionals," the veteran proclaimers of the gospel. But as early as Acts 8 we find that it was not only the apostles but the lay missionaries, those evicted from Jerusalem due to persecution following the martyrdom of Stephen, who carried the gospel to the outlying regions.[11]

When Jesus commanded, "Go ye therefore . . ." He was not just commissioning full-time missionaries. He was commissioning me, you, your family—*the entire church*—into evangelistic service. If we are disciples of the Lord Jesus Christ, and we are, then *our primary work on earth is to implement our Lord's foremost wish of seeking the lost*. Soul-winning must be woven into the very fabric of our family's lifestyle and mind-set. Even small children can be taught witnessing techniques and the importance of interceding daily for missionaries around the world and in our own nation.

We must not wait for a voice from Heaven to tell us to go. *We already have been told to go!* (See Matthew 28:19; Mark 16:15; Acts 1:8.) The late Keith Green aptly said:

> . . . if you don't go, you need a specific calling from God to stay home. Has God definitely told you *not* to "go" somewhere outside your country to preach the gospel? If He hasn't, then you'd better start praying WHERE to go, instead of IF you should go—for again, *you're already called!*[12]

When Jesus calls us to discipleship, He simultaneously calls us to identify with and carry out His mission—spreading the gospel to a lost world. Exemptions to service are not granted for personal convenience. If some Israelites of old had said to Joshua, "We can't go to battle," Joshua immediately would have said, "Prove why you cannot go or you cannot be excused from service." The same rule applies to spiritual service. Every able-bodied Christian should accept his or her duty to reach out with the gospel however God directs *and should especially consider Christian service in a foreign land unless specifically led to stay home.*

Excuse #2: "There Are Already Hundreds of Missionaries . . . We Don't Need Any More"

Nothing could be further from the truth. For example, in North Africa there is one missionary for every two million people. If the situation were proportionally the same in the United States and Canada, we would have about 120 full-time Christian workers and seven small churches to choose from.[13] With only eighty thousand Protestant foreign missionaries, many of whom are in church-nurture ministries, thousands more are needed to penetrate the many unreached people in the frontiers of our world.[14]

In spite of herculean efforts during the last two centuries, large areas of the world remain without the gospel of Christ. The global Christian/non-Christian ratio is very sobering. Twenty-five years ago Christians comprised 33 percent of the world's population; today the ratio is below 30 percent.[15] The scope of our task (especially in Asia) is well expressed in the sedate analysis of Herbert Kane:

> We have been commanded by our Lord to go into all the world, to preach the gospel to every creature, and to make disciples of all nations. It is fair to ask: After two thousand years, how are we doing? Are we forging ahead? Are we standing still? Or are we falling behind?
>
> The population of the world stands today at about 4.8 billion. Of this number, some 1.4 billion adhere to some form of the

Christian faith—Catholic, Orthodox, or Protestant. This leaves 3.4 billion who are still non-Christians, the largest groups being Hindus, Buddhists, and Muslims, most of whom live in the teeming continent of Asia.

Roman Catholic missionaries have been working in Asia for five hundred years and Protestant missionaries have been there for almost two hundred years. Yet only 3 percent of the people are Christians. This leaves 97 percent still to be won to faith in Christ. It is a sobering fact that there are more non-Christians in India and China than there are in [the rest of] the entire world![16]

Dr. Daniel Bacon, USA Home Director for Overseas Missionary Fellowship, summarizes world need from another point of view:

> An estimated 2.4 billion people are living in geographic or cultural contexts where Christ is practically unknown. Some 800 million Muslims follow the teachings of the Koran rather than the Bible. Over 600 million Hindus and 300 million Buddhists are caught up in systems that exclude the living Savior. Well over 200 million animists worship spirits rather than the true and only Creator God. In spite of massive evangelistic efforts in the century, still an estimated 16,000 people groups are unreached.
>
> In addition, the Bible is not available yet to some 3,000 people groups. And even where the Scriptures have been translated, illiteracy prevents many from reading, or the scarcity of Bibles makes it an unknown book.[17]

In view of the facts, Excuse # 2 is indefensible.

Excuse #3: "My Mission Field Is Right Here in America"

I have found the term *mission field* used far too loosely in much Christian vocabulary. *Mission field* is properly applied to a place that has had limited exposure to the gospel or none at all. With this definition, America cannot be considered a true mission field, though of course there are many thousands who need to be won to Christ. Spiritual honesty will force us to admit that there is much greater need in Third-World countries. Oswald Smith has provocatively stated, "No one has the right to hear the gospel twice, while there remains someone who has not heard it once."[18]

There is much work to be done. After two thousand years of mission work, three billion unreached people still need to hear the gospel, many of whom have never seen a Bible, met a single Christian, or even heard the name of Jesus. It is our job as Christians to reach them.

Excuse #4: "I Have So Many Other Things to Do—Making a Living, Raising My Family, and Participating in My Local Church"

These are all laudable goals, but they do not give the whole picture of Christian responsibility. *A family that fervently and prayerfully participates in the Great Commission will win souls!* If by the power of the Holy Spirit you lead men to Christ, you will depart this world with a sense of real accomplishment, even if you leave a thousand other things undone.

Once Jesus called out to a man saying, "Follow me." The man offered the excuse, "Lord, first let me go and bury my father." Jesus said, "Let the dead bury their own dead" (Luke 9:59, 60). By that He meant that there will always be enough spiritually dead people to bury the physically dead. Jesus was not forbidding His followers to attend funerals. His point was that *we should let spiritual priorities occupy our time on earth*. Burying the dead is a good work, but it is a task more compatible to the spiritually dead around us. We cannot do everything, so we should at least do that for which we have been sent. Jesus clarified to the man concerned about his dead father what that primary task is: ". . . you go and proclaim the kingdom of God." A Christian's first responsibility should always be the expansion of the Kingdom of God.

There are many good activities a Christian can engage in on earth, but one is absolutely indispensable—making disciples. The only way souls can come to Christ is by hearing the gospel. But "How, then, can they call on the one they have not believed in? And how can they believe in the one of whom they have not heard? And how can they hear without someone preaching to them?" (Romans 10:14). If Christians do not "Go" and preach Christ, who will? If we do not commend Christ to others, who will? Will the U.S. Congress ever pass legislation requiring the evangelization of the world? Will businesses and corporations take on this task? Or even the Red Cross? Of course not! And just as well, for they are not the proper agents. The church of the Lord Jesus Christ must go forth with the gospel. We and our families are part of the Body of Christ, the church. It is fitting that we personally apply an old adage to our concern about the proclamation of the gospel: "If not you, who? If not now, when?"

While some Christians attend to the work of the Great Commission with great devotion, many are hampered by self-preoccupation or apathy. The "ministries" of introspective Christians continually revolve around themselves and their localized concerns. Like fat, bloated sheep, they have little mission or active service beyond their own needs. At the core of the problem is a comfortable selfishness that refuses to heed the command of Christ to "Go!" This spiritual illness cripples a Christian, keeping him from growing into maturity.

Nothing assists our demonic enemies more than an apathetic Christian. Every man in Christ's army that is not active, well-informed, well-trained, and ready for battle hurts the cause. We must work while it is still light, for "Night is coming, when no one can work" (John 9:4). *We have a whole world to win for Christ!* The odds seem overwhelming, but so it appeared to the first disciples as well. Comments Michael Green:

> It was a small group of eleven men whom Jesus commissioned to carry on his work, and bring the gospel to the whole world. They were not distinguished; they were not well educated; they had no influential backers. In their own nation they were nobodies and, in any case, their own nation was a mere second-class province on the eastern extremity of the Roman map. If they had stopped to weigh

What? My Family Missionaries?

up the probabilities of succeeding in their mission, even granted their conviction that Jesus was alive and that his Spirit went with them to equip them for their task, their hearts must surely have sunk, so heavily were the odds weighted against them. How could they possibly succeed? *And yet they did!*[19]

Church history teaches us that successful evangelistic endeavors lie in the hands of a faithful few who are willing to serve Christ no matter what the cost. May we and our families be counted in that number.

Excuse #5: "Mission Work Is Just Not My Thing— Besides, I Don't Like Interfering in the Lives of Others"

If we don't make an attempt to reach the lost and bring them into God's Kingdom, we are condoning their residency in Hell. If the followers of Christ don't reach them, Satan surely will. As Christians, our allegiance to the Lord Jesus Christ demands that we plunder Hell and populate Heaven!

Some say, "I don't know my Bible well enough to witness." Others are afraid they will get tongue-tied. But if we practice our gospel presentation as seriously as we watch TV or practice our golf stroke or tennis serve, we will be fluent witnesses indeed.

Still others feel aggressive evangelism is a sort of religious imperialism that meddles in the lives of others. If we see a man standing unaware in the path of a speeding car, do we warn him, or do we walk on not wishing to interfere with his life? To ignore his plight would be morally criminal. We have been sent by Almighty God, and where He sends we have a right to go. When the postman knocks on our door to deliver a letter or package, do we blurt out, "How dare you come to my house and invade my privacy"? Of course not. We know he is there as a representative of the U.S. Post Office, and we do not blame him for doing what he was sent to do. As Christians it is our duty to rouse heathen around the globe with an appropriate warning or invitation. Jesus Himself has sent us!

Excuse #6: "I Give to Missions in Lieu of My Personal Involvement"

We should give generously to missions, but that is not a legitimate substitute for personal involvement. Giving and personal involvement are not mutually exclusive.

Excuse #7: "Getting My Family Involved in Missions Can Be Financially Costly—Besides, the Mission Field Can Be Dangerous"

It is true that servitude in foreign missions may entail certain risks. This is part of the cost of discipleship (Mark 8:34, 35). Jesus did not say, "Stay ye therefore, and be ye comfortable and safe. Lo, I am with you always!" No! He commanded us to "Go"! This must be our daily and continual resolve.

Will not God take care of His obedient servants, financially and otherwise? Will He ever send us out without equipping us for the task and providing all our daily necessities? He promises that if we put His Kingdom first, He will take care of all our needs.[20] Obedience to the Great Commission demands faith and trust in the all-knowing, all-loving God who sends us forth. (Appendix C gives further information on why and how Christians should "Go"!)

Guiding Principle:

Refusing to take the easy way out, rejecting all rationalizations which excuse non-obedience to the Great Commission, radical Christian families are ready to serve the Master wherever and however He asks!

ELEVEN

Mission Options for Your Family

Perhaps we and our families are interested in becoming involved in missions. What are some of the ways we can serve in this way?

SHORT-TERM MISSIONS—
A WAY EVERY FAMILY CAN PARTICIPATE

Now that we clearly understand Christ's command to "'Go,'" we may be thinking, "I can't possibly do that! I have a family to take care of!" Traditionally, the way to serve as a foreign missionary has been to live and work among the people in their land, learning their language and customs. This is a highly commendable work. Clearly we need more families to prayerfully consider such a path.

But not all missionaries move overseas and engage in full-time ministry. Our Lord is too creative, and the Body of Christ is too diverse, for this to be the only way. There are many new foreign mission forms, most of which do not necessitate formal seminary training, ecclesiastical approval, or the laborious task of learning a foreign language.

One creative missionary method is that of *making short-term trips to assist local missionaries in their work.* Short-term missionary work dates back to the days of Jesus' sending out the twelve, or even the Apostle Paul's stepping onto a ship for his first missionary journey. *Short-term* can mean anything from a few days to several years. Such trips can be extremely productive and can bring missionaries much encouragement. There are a wide variety of opportunities in hundreds of countries. Students, young adults, whole families, and retired persons from many countries and churches are working through short-term missions to take Christ's gospel to a lost world.

The growth of short-term missions has been phenomenal. Between 1965 and 1975 twenty-three thousand North American short-term workers served overseas. By contrast, between 1975 and 1985 over 248,000 North American short-term workers went to the field, and the numbers continue to escalate.[1] Every year short-termers fan out across the globe to pass out millions of tracts to the unsaved, witness in the streets, preach and teach God's Word, build airfields, construct new churches, wrap miles of bandages around refugees' wounds, start Bible camps, and help in mission hospitals. Many learn to worship to the sound of drums, flutes and tribal chants. All of them come back changed people.

Youth With A Mission (YWAM) and Short Term Evangelical Missions (STEM) are excellent short-term mission organizations, and there are many others as well. (Don't let the word "Youth" in YWAM throw you. Adults and families are more than welcome and help round out the teams.)

YWAM utilizes a three-pronged approach for taking the gospel to the world—Evangelism, Training, and Mercy Ministries. YWAM works in well-organized teams, which may be small or large, mobile or localized. These teams include short-term volunteers and long-term staff and work in cooperation with local churches and sister organizations. Each year fifty thousand people are involved in YWAM's short-term outreach and training. Mobile ministries have gone to 214 countries, while six thousand work as permanent staff in 274 ministry locations in a hundred nations. Workers raise their own financial support from individual churches and friends. No one in Youth With A Mission receives a salary; everyone from the newest volunteer to the international president is responsible for his or her basic support.[2] That's dedication! The point they all have in common is a overriding desire to serve God by winning the lost. Your family can have a part in this too. For more information write or call:

YWAM
300 Vanderbilt Motor Parkway
Hauppauge, NY 11788
(516) 273-5050

Short Term Evangelical Missions is another excellent organization. Every short-term mission team STEM sends out is led by a trained, Christ-centered team leader. This ministry is expert at working with first-time missionaries, even those who have never traveled outside the United States. On an average trip the cost (per person) is about $250 plus airfare. This could be the best $250 you ever spent and would give you far more satisfaction than electronic gadgetry which quickly becomes obsolete, a soon-to-bore video collection, a trip to Disneyland, or one year's Christmas presents. STEM has short-term mission teams going overseas almost every month of the year. They can be contacted at:

STEM Ministries
P.O. Box 290066
Minneapolis, MN 55429
(612) 566-0087

World Christian Teams (WCT) is oriented to college or church groups. They have helped more than 3,500 Christians go overseas on short-term assignments in the past few years. If your church would like help in making a short-term mission trip, call or write:

World Christian Teams
P.O. Box 40010
Pasadena, CA 91104
(818) 797-1907

For more information about other short-term mission organizations (there are many) send for a copy of *Stepping Out,* one of the most comprehensive manuals on the subject. Write to:

Stepping Out
P.O. Box 1668
Evanston, IL 60204

ARE SHORT-TERM MISSIONARY TRIPS EFFECTIVE?

When people "Go" on short-term missions trips, buildings get built, people get healed, and hungry souls are fed the gospel of Jesus Christ. Who goes on these trips? Ordinary people like you and me. They are young and old, skilled and unskilled, average and rich, individuals and families—but they all have a deep interest in sharing the gospel of Jesus Christ. Many are using their only two weeks of paid vacation or a precious school break to go overseas to serve the Lord. What can one do in just two weeks? Here's how one short-term mission organization describes it:

> Using interpreters and local pastors whenever possible, your team will help to plant, water and harvest the seeds of salvation in Jesus Christ with the "foreigners" or national people. Your team will also share in various construction, medical and teaching projects . . . in short, you'll be doing the same things that real missionaries do!
> . . . On a 2-week mission trip, you may be involved in several of these projects:
> - Teaching children
> - Administering basic first-aid
> - Building a church, school, medical facility or similar construction
> - Sharing the gospel of Jesus
> - Assisting full-time missionaries with their work
> - Wiring or plumbing a building
> - Leading a Bible study or preaching a sermo
> - Teaching basic health and hygiene

- Praying with others and praying for others
- Conducting an "impromptu" medical clinic
- Leading people to Christ
- Learning what it takes and what it costs to become a missionary.[3]

Do these things sound like they promote valuable assistance to the Kingdom of God? Having been on several short-term mission trips myself, I can personally vouch for their effectiveness. Equally important is the life-changing impact they have on the individual or family who endeavors to serve Christ by giving of themselves in this way. Nothing helps give excitement and vision for ministry quite like overseas exposure, even if only for two or three weeks.

Are you afraid of going to a dangerous country? Then start with a short-term mission trip to Europe, or neighboring countries such as Mexico, Jamaica, or the Dominican Republic. Each has a great need for gospel workers, and the jittery short-term missionary will experience little culture shock in such lands. As confidence increases, so will the desire to minister in more poverty-stricken, gospel-destitute countries. For an overview of short-term mission opportunities see Appendix C.

You may object, "But we have small children in our family!" Short-term trips can start with just Dad, or Dad and Mom. Christian friends interested in gospel outreach can watch your children on a short-term basis. Saving money for future trips will allow children to travel along when they are ready. But this will not happen accidentally—you must plan for it! There is nothing more exciting and thrilling than for a family to travel abroad together to share the Good News of Jesus Christ.

TENTMAKING MISSIONARIES

Another method of missionary service is "tentmaking ministry." Used by the Apostle Paul two thousand years ago, tentmaking remains a highly successful method of mission work. If we had more tentmakers abroad, modern Christianity would have far greater success in breaking down the walls of heathenism, for tentmaking ministry is the chief method of getting the gospel into countries with restricted access.

A tentmaker may be defined as "a committed Christian with marketable skills who lives and works outside his own country for the express purpose of using those skills as a means of gaining opportunities for sharing his faith in Jesus Christ."[4] Tentmaker missionaries are ordinary people with an extraordinary desire to reach people with the gospel. There are many open doors worldwide for tentmaking skills as physicians, dentists, educators, corporate executives and advisors, military personnel, engineers, scientists, researchers, construction workers, health care workers, English language teachers, social services, and many other fields.

Tentmaking requires spiritual, mental and physical preparation. But if you have a passion for lost souls, there are good organizations ready to assist you in making the right contacts. Some twenty-three thousand companies have employees overseas, but finding them is not always easy.

Tentmakers International is a service agency dedicated singularly to mobilizing tentmaking advocates, preparing and placing tentmaker candidates, and nurturing overseas tentmakers. TI offers an extensive database of thousands of current job openings, as well as a quarterly newsletter entitled *Tentmaking Today*. The newsletter contains personal stories about tentmakers, reports on various countries, job opportunities overseas, and tentmaker preparation. If you're interested in exploring the tentmaking option, you can write for TI's *Resource Guide* or their twenty-minute VHS video *Operation Tentmaker*, which gives an introduction to tentmaking. If you are interested in using your skills as a tentmaker, call or write:

Tentmakers International
P.O. Box 33836
Seattle, WA 98133
(206) 546-8411

Another resource and service organization carrying an extensive database of overseas jobs is Intercristo. Intercristo works exclusively with non-profit, Christian organizations. In its twenty-year history, Intercristo (itself a Christian non-profit ministry) has helped over 150,000 Christians nationally in career placement and over ten thousand Christian ministries in recruiting personnel. Their computerized network provides each applicant with job leads that personally match their skills, education, and background with more than twenty-five thousand current job openings in over twelve hundred Christian organizations in the U.S. and abroad. Call or write:

Intercristo
19303 Fremont Ave. North
Seattle, WA 98133
(800) 426-1343

TI and Intercristo are not employment agencies, but job referral services. For a small fee (usually under fifty dollars) they will make multiple job searches based on a person's qualifications. We need more tentmakers, and you may be one of them. Tentmaking can be rewarding and and extremely fruitful to those bold enough to make it a reality in their lives.

ASSISTING IN FOREIGN CRUSADES

Another option for missionary service is involvement in foreign crusade work. A large number of counselors and follow-up personnel are needed to minister to those converted at crusade meetings. Evangelist Reinhard Bonnke (one of several possibilities) periodically invites lay involvement in his African crusades. We can thus witness for ourselves the harvest of souls in Africa, and as an added benefit see some spectacular scenery on that continent. In the last two years more than two million souls in Africa have come into God's Kingdom through the ministry of Reinhard Bonnke. Whole cities bound by witchcraft are being set free through the power of the gospel. Such Christian service experience is invaluable. Willing Christians are needed for ushering, counseling and intercession. For information write:

Reinhard Bonnke Ministries, Inc.
P.O. Box 3851
Laguna Hills, CA 92654
(714) 586-2440

No matter which way we go—short-term, tentmaking, or crusade assistance—mission opportunities abound for all who are willing to serve the Lord with their whole heart. *The key requirement is a sold-out-for-Jesus commitment.* There is verity in the old adage, "If there is a will, there is a way." If we have a desire to sacrificially give of ourselves to fulfill the Great Commission, there are plenty of ways to do it.

WORLD MISSIONS AT YOUR DOORSTEP

We should also seriously consider reaching out to the mission field that is literally at our doorsteps. There are foreign students studying in colleges and universities all over the United States. It is estimated that 25 to 50 percent of these international students will become leaders when they return to their native countries. The bitter truth is that most of these 370,000 foreign students from 180 nations will go back to their mother country without any person having ever told them about Jesus.[5] Being an American is not a sin, but being an American and not reaching the world for Christ is a sin. We can invite international students into our homes, get to know them, share with them, love them, explain the central teachings of the Bible to them, take them to church with us, and win them to Jesus!

Guiding Principle:

Committed Christian families will do all they can to be aware of missionary opportunities available to them and will trust God to show them which doors to walk through, for His glory.

START EARLY

We ought to teach our children from their youngest years to think about missions. As a young boy of twelve Jesus said, "Knew ye not that I must be about my Father's business?" (Luke 2:49, KJV). Young children should be reared early on to ask, "Lord, what would You have me to do?"

There are a number of ways we can promote a predominant mission-mindedness in our families. First, family mission zeal can be inspired by reading books and listening to tapes about great missionaries. Christian bookstores and Bible college libraries are teeming with the works of missionaries—their travels and their adventures. This is some of the most exciting literature in the world—almost a lifetime of reading. We may be unable to absorb all these books, but reading a few of them will vastly increase our love for mission work.

Good sources for missionary books include:

World Missions Book Club
c/o William Carey Library
P.O. Box 40129
Pasadena, CA 91104
(818) 798-0819

New Hope Press
Box 11657
Birmingham, AL 35202
(205) 991-8100

Frontline Communications
P.O. Box 55787
Seattle, WA 98155

Crown Magnetics offers taped stories of such missionary heroes as David Livingstone and Adoniram Judson. For information call or write:

Crown Magnetics
650 N. 6th Street
Lebanon, PA 17042
(800) PA2-3008 inside PA
(800) USA-2008—outside PA

Teen Missions International is an exciting and comprehensive missions program especially for teens and preteens. Teen Missions offers a boot camp designed to help young people develop an early interest and involvement in missions. Their intensive physical/spiritual training program and no-dating policy makes Teen Missions a real winner. Your teenager is guaranteed to return home a different and better person. Areas of training include: cultural conditioning, personal evangelism, construction, Bible memory, and singing. Teens will hear vivid testimonials from experienced missionaries as well as from returning students. They also receive teaching on subjects such as daily devotions, controlling the tongue, the balanced life, attitude towards parents, living with others, daily devotions, finances, tithing, saving, saying no to peer pressure, and many other areas. For information contact:

Teen Missions International, Inc.
885 East Hall Road
Merritt Island, FL 32953-8418
(305) 453-0350

This is an excellent way to introduce adolescents and preteens to mission work too. My daughter went to Teen Missions' boot camp and gained a whole new outlook on missions. There are many other organizations and camps available as well. The important thing is to start early and be creative!

Second, we can establish missions savings accounts for ourselves and for each of our children. If 10 percent of American Christians got serious about this, and starting making short-term mission trips as well, the church would experience spiritual revolution. By using missions savings accounts, by the time your children graduate from high school they will have enough saved to engage in one or two years of full-time foreign mission work.

Mormon families are committed to involving their children in a twelve- to twenty-four-month missionary stint. The parents start saving for their children's missionary service while they are small. Over twenty-six thousand Mormons are currently engaged in missions in over ninety countries. Are Mormon missionary stints effective? Half a million South Americans have recently become Mormon. In Peru, nine hundred people convert to Mormonism every month. Thirty-one out of every one thousand babies born in Brazil are born to Mormon parents. Mormon work continues in in the Far East in countries such as Japan and the Philippines (with some ninety thousand Mormons), and in Iron Curtain countries such as East Germany (with some four thousand Mormons).[6]

Mormon efforts in encouraging their young (early twenties) to participate in missionary service is paying off big. And if they can do it, evangelical Christians can do the same—even more so. We have a gospel so rich in grace, it ought to be shouted to the multitudes! We don't promote a doctrine of works-righteousness or a spiritual fantasy that one can become a god (the Mormon doctrine of Eternal Progression). Nor do we teach Biblically absurd dogmas such as baptism of the dead, secret temple rites, or everlasting marriages (Eternal Sealing). Ours is the simple gospel revealed in the sixty-six canonical books of God's Word. We believe, teach and confess that we are saved exclusively by grace, through faith in the blood atonement of our Lord Jesus Christ. *There is no other way!* We Christians who have the true message of salvation must fully support mission activity among our young adults.

Considering the current state of American colleges and universities, parents should reevaluate those institutions' net worth. Why invest a small fortune in a learning environment that is saturated with humanism and immorality? Even if our children feel they must obtain a college degree in order to meet a certain life goal, why not go about it a little differently? If Christian parents want to get radical, they should encourage their children to spend one year, or at least a summer, on a short-term mission trip before they go to college. This will dramatically change their way of thinking and constructively help shape their view of life. After that, we can encourage them to attend a Bible college for at least a year, where they will become firmly rooted and grounded in Bible doctrine and Christian polemics. This will give them a strong foundation that would help them survive the sea of degeneracy found at secular universities.

Third, early training includes a parental model of daily fervent prayer for God's work around the world. Our children should hear us ask God how our families can get personally involved. We need more harvesters (Matthew 9:37, 38). Dads should lead in making evangelistic prayer a way of life in the family. Pray for the various countries and their specific gospel needs. An excellent tool which augments a commitment to evangelistic prayer is a book entitled *Operation World* by Patrick Johnstone. *Operation World* provides comprehensive information about foreign countries, including their population, people, economy, politics, dominant religion, and specific prayer needs for the Christian work going on there. A world prayer map is available from the same supplier. Get your whole family involved in praying for world outreach. You can order *Operation World* (approximately $7.00) and the *World Prayer Map* (approximately $3.00) from:

STL Publications
2 Industrial Park Road
Waynesboro, GA 30830

Christian parents are meant to raise godly, Biblically-literate, mission-minded children. There is no time to squander. We must be passionate about our Father's business in a labor of love.

Guiding Principle:
Radical Christian parents see the importance of family zeal for missions, teach their children to win others to Christ, and help the family work together to serve the Lord as His witnesses.

WHAT IS YOUR FAMILY PERSONALLY DOING FOR MISSIONS?

The consequences of evangelistic neglect are serious, affecting both us and our families. Such impoverishment deprives us of the deepest relationship we can have with Christ Jesus; it polarizes us from the primary purpose of God; it robs us of the deepest experiences of the Holy Spirit; it denies us many of the joys and blessings the Lord provides.

There is no substitute for personal involvement. We must realize that we are not our own, but have been bought with a price (1 Corinthians 6:19, 20). While financial support for missions is important, no amount of giving can compensate for personal labor for the Lord Jesus Christ.

The measure of our seriousness is evident by our fruit. Imagine that there is a large fruit plantation in your region of the country. The owner has invested millions of dollars in the groves, soil development, irrigation, fertilizer, mechanical fruit-pickers, and labor force. The intended fruit production promises to be the best in the world. After years of tender loving care, the orchards are mature and ready for peak productivity. The owner comes by to inspect the fruit and size up his investment. He asks the operations manager, "How many tons of fruit do you expect this year?" The operations manager replies, "None!" "None!" the owner cries out. "Why not? I've been investing in this project for years. I expect results." The manager says, "The trees have no fruit, sir, but look how beautiful and lush they are. Observe how rich the soil is. And don't forget, we employ hundreds of satisfied workers." "But when do you expect fruit production?" asks the angry owner. "I just don't know!" replies the operations manager. "Perhaps never!"

Obviously the owner has a right to be upset, for the exclusive purpose of the orchard is to produce fruit. Since there is no fruit, his investment has been wasted. God has invested in us. He wants us to produce fruit, to "go and make disciples" (see Matthew 28:19, 20; John 15:8; Romans 7:4; 1 Corinthians 3:13, 14.; cf. Isaiah 5:1-7). God's people are forgiven and filled with the Holy Spirit for a reason—to glorify

God. And our Heavenly Father tells us how we can best glorify Him—He wants us to make disciples. Consequently, should we not energetically seek out the most fertile fields and put our best efforts into reaping a plentiful harvest for the Lord Jesus Christ?

What if a farmer went out to a smooth, fallow field, a field that had never been plowed or seeded? Without cultivating or sowing, he prays over it saying, "Lord, I thank You for the crop this land will soon produce. I just know You are going to bring me a crop of wheat." In a few days the farmer goes out, but nothing has come up. So he prays some more: "Lord, I really want a harvest. I know You desire it and even command it. I too want it." Still nothing happens! He begins to yearn for a crop. He even weeps and fasts for it. Still nothing happens! He yells at the top of his lungs, "My God is a miracle-working God. He's going to bring a harvest." But obviously He isn't, for the farmer has not carried out his responsibilities. Similarly, God abides by the principle of gospel proclamation He Himself has established: *If you don't go out and sow seed, you can't expect a crop.*

We can pray, yearn, weep, fast, and recognize the need. But if we don't sow the Word of God in the hearts of unregenerate people, we cannot expect results. We can go to church and yell out, "My God is a miracle-working God. He desires that none be lost, but that all come to a knowledge of the truth. I believe that people are going to get converted right now all over the world." But if that is all we are doing, the multitudes are not going to come to Christ! God works according to His Word, and His Word tells us He has appointed His followers to be His agents for getting the message out so the spiritually impoverished masses can be saved. Not even the angels of Heaven have such a privilege.

True Christianity multiplies itself. What power there is in this. When the Word is planted, God promises, it will produce a crop (Isaiah 55:10, 11). Which would you rather have—a million dollars a day for thirty-two days or a penny doubled each day for thirty-two days? The latter choice yields the most. The same principle applies to spiritual multiplication. Consider these challenging words by Stephen Olford:

> Have you ever thought of the difference it would make to the true Church if every Christian won three souls to Christ each year? Consider this mathematically for a moment. If there were only five thousand Christians in the world, and each one led three souls to Christ in a year (and each succeeding year), and also taught his converts to do the same—in one year there would be twenty thousand Christians; in nine years there would be over one thousand millions; and in ten years the whole of the known world would be evangelized![7]

Effective discipling produces exponential growth (Mark 4:8). If you plant a kernel of corn, it will grow into a stalk. A healthy cornstalk should yield two or three good ears of corn. Each ear of corn can contain over a hundred new kernels good for resowing. Even if two-thirds of the kernels do not germinate, there would be a continual increase in the volume of corn produced year after year. Effective, evangelistic, globally-minded Christianity will grow in a similar fashion.

The wrench in the works are Christians who are not spiritually reproductive. This sabotages the evangelistic plan of our Lord. Commenting on this, Robert E. Coleman says:

> His whole evangelistic strategy—indeed, the fulfillment of His very purpose in coming into the world, dying on the cross, and rising from the grave—depended upon the faithfulness of His chosen disciples to this task. It did not matter how small the group was to start with so long as they reproduced and taught their disciples to reproduce. This was the way His Church was to win—through the dedicated lives of those who knew the Savior so well that His Spirit and method constrained them to tell others. As simple as it may seem, this was the way the gospel would conquer. He had no other plan.

... No wonder Jesus so indelibly impressed upon His disciples the necessity and inevitability of His life reproducing its kind. An illustration of this was the parable of the vine and the branches (John 15:1-17). Here in one of the most simple yet profound analogies of the Lord, Christ explained that the purpose of both the vine (Himself) and the branches (believers in Him) was to bear fruit. Hence, any branch that did not yield produce was cut off by the husbandman—it was worthless. What is more, those branches which did not produce were pruned by the husbandman that they might yield more fruit (John 15:2). It was clear that the life-sustaining power of the vine was not to be bestowed endlessly upon lifeless branches. Any branch that lived on the vine had to produce to survive, for that was its intended nature. Jesus then made the application to His disciples. As surely as they were participants in His life, even so they would bear His fruit (John 15:5, 8), and furthermore, their fruit would remain (John 15:16). A barren Christian is a contradiction. A tree is known by its fruit.[8]

We should each make a quick check of our personal spiritual fruit production. How many people have we led to the Lord Jesus Christ in the past year? In the past three years? The past five? In what ways have we actively sought to promote righteousness in our families? In our communities? In our country? Such fruit production is a sign of mature Christianity. Christians who live in cultural ease, who rarely win souls, who never undertake battle on the front lines, will one day realize how much they squandered opportunities to carry out their share of the Master's work.

Training our families in effective soul-winning is the greatest service we can offer Christ in this life. No Christian should appear before the Lord empty-handed. Personal involvement—fruitful service—is the best demonstration of our love for God. It must be the heart and center of our family life as well. Soul-winning parents are a thousand times more likely to have soul-winning children, just as the most effective foreign missionaries come from soul-winning churches. We must pray that our families develop a sold-out-for-Jesus commitment. We must fervently ask God to help our families be part of reaping a big spiritual harvest. Our goal is world conquest, and we should work for results. This is the sign of a flourishing family.

TWELVE

Conclusion: The Essence of a Flourishing Family

We have discussed how a radical Christian life will alter our priorities, our lifestyle, how we spend our time, how we think, how we speak, how we dress, the company we keep, and the way we raise our children. Becoming a Christian is a radical spiritual transformation, and so is the change from mediocre Christianity to becoming radical New Testament disciples of Jesus Christ. *God wants our whole family to fully exhibit Christian radicalism, devoted commitment, wholehearted zeal, a state of spiritual non-compromise. This is the essence of a flourishing family.*

Jesus calls His followers to change the world they live in and to leave a lasting impact upon it. He commands us to be confrontational with the truth of God. *For the radical New Testament Christian, it is never business as usual!* There is much to do and only one lifetime in which to do it. "Teach us to number our days aright, that we may gain a heart of wisdom" (Psalm 90:12). The world must be touched by the true Light of the world, Jesus Christ. Making His saving grace and perfect will known is the goal and purpose of our very existence.

EVERY FAMILY MAKES A CHOICE

Every Christian family must choose between two kinds of lifestyles. The first has fruit which is a *permanent memorial* to Jesus Christ. It is characterized by being productive, obedient, content, and filled with joy. The fruit of the second lifestyle is like a *sand castle*. It looks great, but it does not last. Though some Christians expend a great deal of religious effort and have many good intentions, their life is characterized by spiritual mediocrity, lukewarmness, low resistance to temptation, discontent, worry, and low spiritual productivity.

The first lifestyle is not arrived at haphazardly. It is a clear, conscious, determined choice in cooperation with the Holy Spirit. It is setting our face like flint against all obstacles that get in the way of our love and service to Jesus Christ. Radical Christianity exceeds religiosity. We can attend church and Bible class, receive Holy Communion, serve on a church board or committee, be active in church groups, and yet not be a radical Christian family. A radical Christian family gives indisputable priority to Jesus Christ and His will for their lives. This is evident in their attitudes and goals, the way they spend their time and money, their life testimony and witness (fruit). It means being a family after God's own heart, a family whose priorities are God's priorities, whose choices are God's choices, whose conversation, activities and deeds are pleasing to God.

Franky Schaeffer described the two choices in this manner:

> . . . the very hinge of fate and the destiny of not only ourselves but also our children depends upon which course we choose. To *not* think about these issues and to not take a stand is also an activist approach. It is actively passive, giving over the field to the devil and his emissaries: Christians in the act of surrender, running from the scene of battle, coats flapping, foolish smiles on our faces, attempting to save our own hides at any cost. How much better to take our stand in this generation with the saints who have stood before and to affirm the following statement:
>
> "Therefore, seeing we also are surrounded by so great a cloud of witnesses, let us lay aside every weight, and the sin which so easily ensnares us, and let us run with endurance the race that is set before us, looking to Jesus, the author and finisher of our faith, who

for the joy that was set before Him endured the cross, despising the shame, and has sat down at the right hand of the throne of God. For consider Him who endured such hostility from sinners against Himself, lest you become weary and discouraged in your minds." (Hebrews 12:1-3)[1]

Our lives and our families can be permanent memorials for Almighty God or sand castles whose works are soon erased. We can let our lives and witness etch their eternal mark in God's master plan, or we can expend our efforts building short-lived earthly empires. Are our families lukewarm or red-hot for Jesus? What does our lifestyle reveal about our spiritual commitment? The radical, New Testament Christian family is both salty and illuminating! This is the way of life most pleasing to God—and the most rewarding. The choice is ours.

APPENDIX A
Home Education Resources

HOME SCHOOLING SUPPORT ORGANIZATIONS

If you would like more information about the home school support organization in your state, call or write the National Center for Home Education and request the name and address of the home school organization in your state.

National Center for Home Education
P.O. Box 125
Paeonian Springs, VA 22129
(703) 882-4770

BASIC PRIMER ON HOME SCHOOLING

Ray E. Ballmann, *The How and Why of Home Schooling* (Wheaton, IL: Crossway Books, 1987). Everything you need to know to start home schooling. It also helps veteran home schoolers stay committed and motivated. Available from your local Christian bookstore or write:

Foundation for Family Development
P.O. Box 6453
Fort Worth, TX 76115
($9.95 plus $1.00 for postage and handling)

HOME SCHOOL LEGAL ASSISTANCE ORGANIZATION

Home School Legal Defense Association
Paeonian Springs, VA 22129
(703) 882-3838

HOME SCHOOL MAGAZINE

The Teaching Home
P.O. Box 20219
Portland, OR 97220-0219
(503) 253-9633

CORRESPONDENCE COURSES

A Beka Correspondence School
Box 18000
Pensacola, FL 32523-9160
(800) 334-7209

Advanced Training Institute of America
(Institute in Basic Youth Conflicts)
Box 1
Oak Brook, IL 60521
(708) 323-9800

Calvert School
Tuscany Road
Baltimore, MD 21210
(301) 243-6030

Christian Liberty Academy
502 W. Euclid Avenue
Arlington Heights, IL 60004
(708) 259-8736

Hewitt-Moore Child Development Center
P.O. Box 9
Washougal, WA 98671-0009
(206) 835-8708

Seton Home Study School
Dept. C
1 Kidd Lane
Front Royal, VA 23630
(703) 636-9990

Summit Christian Academy
P.O. Box 802041
Dallas, TX 75380
(800) 362-9180

The Sycamore Tree
2179 Meyer Place
Costa Mesa, CA 92627
(714) 650-4466
(This is designed with Roman Catholic families in mind.)

APPENDIX B

Scheduling a Life-changing Seminar in Your Area
"Building an Effective Family Life!"

Many parents and families have found this seminar, offered by the Foundation for Family Development, to be extremely valuable. The subjects covered in this seminar include:

- Principles that facilitate dynamic family leadership, promote marital harmony, encourage peak familial growth and maturity, and put new spark into home life.
- Guidelines for effective Biblical parenting.
- Rules for maximizing our use of time so we can get more things done.
- Insights on how to evaluate our relationship with our culture and the extended family.
- Understanding the role of television in the home.
- Shaping a Christian view of dating.
- Guidelines for developing a godly family that impacts the world in a beneficial way.
- Why home schooling is such an attractive educational option.
- How to build a creative home school and get fathers involved.
- Countering the socialization argument and rendering it meritless.

For information about scheduling a seminar in your area, or if you simply would like to be kept on our mailing list, write or call:

Foundation for Family Development
P.O. Box 6453
Ft. Worth, TX 76115
(817) HIS-WORD (447-9673)

APPENDIX C

Short-term Mission Opportunities

Each year hundreds of young people from North America go to the mission field. Some stay a few weeks, some for several years. They work in every major world area doing every kind of task. All are challenged and forced to grow by this giving of themselves.

The following listing is a sampler of the many opportunities available from which you can choose. As you begin thinking and exploring you'll probably discover many more. It's well worth your time to find the option that best suits your interests, timeframe, and geographical inclination. But beware of a windowshopper mentality. Search for a place in God's short-term work force in readiness to go for it soon!

Name/Address Contact Person	Background of Agency	1991 Short-term Fields	Training Provided
Adventures in Missions 1161 Summerwood Cr. West Palm Beach, FL 33414 407-790-0394 Mr. Seth Barnes	More opportunities exist to reach the world's needy than ever before. AIM has the ministry of bringing the mission field to your doorstep. We do this through our data base of short-term missions opportunities, and our projects for college students and youth groups.	Mexico, Jamaica, Panama, Dominican Rep., Costa Rica, U.S.	Help in how to conduct an effective opportunities research process. Extensive materials and preparation for groups.
Africa Inland Mission P.O. Box 178 Pearl River, NY 10965 914-735-4014 Wade Ewing	AIM concentrates on reaching unreached peoples groups and training national church leaders. Many support ministries are utilized.	Kenya, Tanzania, Zaire, C.A.R., Mozambique, Comoro Islands	Pre-field: Required reading, two day orientation seminar. Field: Conducted by missionary.
Arab World Ministries (AWM) P.O. Box 96 Upper Darby, PA 19082 213-352-2003 Helen Wilson	Founded in 1881. Interdenominational mission to reach Arab Muslims with the Gospel in Europe, North Africa and the Middle East.	France, Holland, London, Tunisia, Morocco, Jordan, Egypt	Pre-field training before departure. Books/articles provided to read.
Celebrant Singers P.O. Box 1416 Visalia, CA 93279 800-321-2500 Wes Rowland	Interdenominational, Spirit-filled missions agency, training and sending out teams of surrendered musicians.	Poland, Bulgaria, Yugoslavia, Hungary, Central America, North America	Intensive 10-day rehearsal and training camp in California. Focus on spiritual equipping/preparation, cross-cultural ministry.
Chosen People Ministries/STEP 6057 N. Kedzie Ave., Chicago, IL 60659-2496 312-338-5959 Mr. Galen Banashak Mr. Roy Schwarcz	Since 1894 Chosen People Ministries (formerly American Board of Missions to the Jews) has proclaimed the Gospel to the Jewish people.	United States and Canada	STEP offers three weeks of classroom training in "Jewish Objections to the Gospel," "Messianic Apologetics," etc. plus hands-on field evangelism.
Christian Encounter Ministries P.O. Box 1022 Grass Valley, CA 95945 916-288-0877 Mike Boon	CEM uses a residential counseling program plus wilderness camping experiences to introduce troubled youth, ages 16–25, to Christ and to the Christian lifestyle. Founded in 1970, CEM is interdenominational and evangelical in thrust. College credit is available for some programs.	Christian Encounter Ranch and Discovery Expeditions (CEM's camping arm) are located in N. California.	Orientation takes place in the midst of hands-on learning and ministry. Each intern receives a training manual, attends weekly group meetings and meets regularly with a full-time faculty member.
A Christian Ministry in the National Parks 222 1/2 E. 49th St. New York, NY 10017 212-758-3450 Warren Ost	Since 1951, ACMNP has extended the mission and ministry of America's churches to the visitors, workers, and residents of National Parks, forests, and resort areas. ACMNP cooperates with National Park Service, park concessioners, denominations.	65 different areas, 23 states, 300 staff worker-priests.	Pre-field: Required attendance at 2-day orientation conference. Conference held in 9 regions throughout United States.
Christian Music/Sports Outreach International 12480 Wayzata Blvd. Minnetonka, MN 55433 612-541-5343 Mr. Jack Isleib	CMOI/CSOI is an interdenominational ministry of Christian Outreach International, organizing teams and lay people for 25-day short-term mission work overseas, evangelizing through the medium of music/sports.	U.K., Sweden, Finland, Germany, Switzerland, Holland, USSR, Poland	Training and orientation camp is held in the States prior to departure, emphasizing practical evangelism and skill development.

Appendix C: Short-term Mission Opportunities

Requirements/ Length of Service	Work Description and Cost
Youth groups must be accompanied by leaders. Accept jr. high through college ages. Projects last one to two weeks.	Projects are designed to help group leaders meet their goal: the spiritual growth of members. Ministry is multi-faceted and includes construction, service and evangelism. Top speakers challenge group members to grow. COST—$700 + air or less for overseas projects.
1) Application procedure. 2) Recommendation of pastor. 3) Medical clearance. 4) Agreement with doctrinal statement. Volunteer: 2–11 months. Short term: 1–3 years.	Live and work with missionaries in varied ministries. Opportunities in construction, maintenance, clerical, medical, education and others. Work with national Christians in most cases. COST—$2500–$3000 for summer program.
College age and older: functional French for France team. Length of service varies: 2-6 week programs.	In Europe, evangelism through literature distribution, open air drama, book stands and films. In North Africa, training and exposure to ministry among Arab Muslims; interaction with field workers and friendship evangelism where possible. COST—$1000–$2000, plus air fare.
Minimum age is 18 (or HS graduate), to 35. Application and audition procedure. Summer, 9-month, and full-time terms.	Music is a powerful tool on the mission field! Emphasis on praise and worship, musical excellence, living in community, "hands on" counseling and personal ministry, and ministering to unreached peoples. COST—$3,295 for entire summer, including training.
Jewish and Gentile believers 18 years or older with a pastor's reference. Length of service ranges from three weeks to six and a half weeks.	After classroom training, teams embark on a "missionary journey" to various U.S. cities doing street work and door-to-door evangelism. COST—(Phase I) $995 (transportation not included). Students accepted for Phase II have their costs covered by by participating Phase II churches.
1) A Christian with a desire to share Christ with others. 2) Completed 2 or more years of college. 3) Willing to work hard and serve others. 4) Complete application procedure. Minimum length of service: 3 months (any time of year).	Live and work in a rural setting with full-time staff and troubled youth. Teaching, discipling, working, doing chores, recreation, camping are all part of the program. COST—You receive free room and board, laundry privileges, and a guaranteed monthly income (we ask you to make an effort to raise support). Travel to California is not covered by CEM.
Vital faith, creativity, maturity, commitment. Able to minister with Christians of other denominations. Singles or married couples, age 20 or older. Must be available for summer through Labor Day, year-long internships available. Participants: Work full-time, are paid by park concession companies, usually earn $750-$1500 after room/board/taxes.	Model Christian lifestyle while living, working with fellow employees. Provide interdenominational services in National Park campgrounds through preaching, music. COST—Transportation to/from park paid by participant.
1) Must be born again. 2) Good music/sports ability. 3) Application procedure. 4) Desire to win souls for the Lord.	Evangelism using music/sports as a tool, reaching out to a wide variety of people in and out of churches. Ministry takes place in public squares, schools, athletic events/concerts. Travel, minister the Gospel, experience personal growth. Daily Bible studies. COST—$1,200–3,600.

Name/Address Contact Person	Background of Agency	1991 Short-term Fields	Training Provided
City Team Ministries P.O. Box 143 San Jose, CA 95103 408-998-4770 Kelli Holland	Glorifying God by serving the urban poor through humanitarian aid, evangelism. Includes camping and sports programs for youth, cross-cultural evangelism, outreach to needy families, homeless. Academic training in cities.	California (San Jose, Santa Cruz, East Palo Alto) and PA (Philadelphia, Chester)	One week cross-cultural urban training, followed by one week of specialized training (i.e., youth, cross-cultural, street evangelism, etc.).
DenSu Ministries, Inc. Box 5 Doylestown, OH 44230 216-658-4991 Fax 216-658-3499 Mr. Dennis Caplinger	Newly formed non-profit ministry committed to helping western believers do New Testament evangelism in the least reached nations. We work closely with Churches in U.S. to send evangelistic teams to the Final Frontiers.	Mongolia, Albania, Thailand, Southeast Asia	No formal training is necessary. Pre-departure orientation is given along with some written and video materials. Spiritual preparation through prayer is the most vital.
Destination SUMMIT ASSIST Program New Tribes Mission Sanford, FL 32771 407-321-6197 John Cross	ASSIST is one of two Destination SUMMIT programs. Work alongside tribal missionaries. Programs are short-term ministries of New Tribes Mission, a fundamental, non-denominational faith mission society, dedicated to reaching tribal people in their own tongue.	Papua New Guinea, West New Britain, Ivory Coast, Senegal, Liberia, Latin America	1 week pre-field preparation at appropriate gate-city-location.
Discipleship Ministries P.O. Box 628 Salunga, PA 17538-0628 717-898-2251	Discipleship Ministries is one of three program departments of Eastern Mennonite Board of Missions and Charities. Three programs with Discipleship Ministries—Voluntary Service (VS), Youth Evangelism Service (YES), and Summer Training Action Teams (STAT)—serve to send youth and young adults to stateside and overseas locations.	Central America, Caribbean, East Africa, France, Spain, Germany, Venezuela, Mexico City, Eastern U.S.	Three week to three month discipleship training precedes outreach.
Eastern European Outreach Box 983 Sun City, CA 92381 800-829-9888	Since 1968, EEO has assisted the people of Eastern Europe with their spiritual and physical needs. Interdenominational; work with churches and mission organizations. Offices in Holland, Germany and the U.S. Extensive Bible distribution; we now also provide greatly needed relief aid.	Ukraine, Latvia, Russia, Siberia, Poland, Romania, Yugoslavia, Hungary, Czechoslovakia	
Far East Broadcasting Company P.O. Box 1 La Mirada, CA 90637 213-947-4651 Richard Love	A non-denominational missionary radio network. We have stations in five countries and Programming offices in 19 countries.	Saipan and Philippines	*Radio Broadcaster Internships*: To gain experience in preparing radio spots, short features, dramas, and program segments. *Electrical Engineer Internships*: To learn all aspects of radio engineering activities.
Field Ministry Internships University of the Nations 75-5851 Kuakina Hwy. Kauila-Kona, HI 96740 John Henry	FMI gives Christian college students from other countries opportunities for cross-cultural experiences related to their major fields of study. Students gain insight into how their fields of study may be used to help minister to the poor and needy.	Belize, Brazil, Guatemala, Haiti, Mexico, Eastern Europe	A one-week pre-departure team orientation. The typical program covers a six-week period and grants five to six semester-equivalent credits.

Appendix C: Short-term Mission Opportunities

Requirements/ Length of Service	Work Description and Cost
Must be a born-again believer active in a church, with a compatible theology to CityTeam's statement of faith. Must be committed to serving the body of Christ and have a teachable spirit. Length of service: June-August.	Youth ministry, camp, sports, evangelism, street ministry, and social work. Support is $975. Also available: International Center for Urban Training. Part of a degree program providing academic and pragmatic exposure. COST—for graduate or undergraduate credit, $3,060. Cost for one-year certificate, $1,480.
1) You must be born again. 2) Pastoral reference. 3) Valid passport. 4) Ability to serve in a group. 5) Finances for trip. Time commitment: Two weeks.	A public demonstration of the Gospel for those who have never heard, through Scripture and literature distribution, along with witnessing and showing the love of Jesus by any and every means. The average 2 week cost is $2,500. Literature and all arrangements are provided.
At least age 15, believer with desire to walk with the Lord. Length of service: 2-4 weeks Jan/Feb or 6-8 weeks Jun/July/Aug.	Assistance to tribal missionaries building airstrips, housing, medical dispensaries, etc. and cross-cultural involvement on teams led by New Tribes Mission missionaries. COST—depending on choice of location, ranges from $1000 to $3000.
Varies by program.	Ministry opportunities—evangelism through witnessing, music, drama, mime and puppets. Service opportunities—secretarial, child-care, classroom aid, home repair, church building, help medical teams. Church opportunities—help in church planting, youth ministry. COST—VS persons receive stipend while living in household. YES: $3,200 to $4,100. STAT: $2,400 to $3,000.
Committed to Jesus Christ, ready to serve and flexible. Short term: 2 wks., min. age 18, travel by bus. Long term: Write for details.	5 to 8 mission trips to Eastern Europe each year. Destinations chosen by greatest need and best opportunities to share Christ. We minister in schools, churches, and hospitals. Many opportunities to share in the streets and squares of towns rarely visited by Westerners. This is the cutting edge of evangelism. COST—$1300 to $2200 for travel, room and board.
Student in junior or senior year of college with career goal to to serve as missionary. *Broadcasters*: Major in Communications. *Electrical Engineers*: Major leading towards a bachelor of science in electrical engineering. Minimum of ten weeks.	Individual will work and learn at stations in Saipan and Philippines under the direction of a senior missionary. COST—Approximately $2,500 which includes air travel, food, housing and utilities.
1) A demonstrated relationship with the Lord Jesus Christ. 2) A junior or senior standing with a declared major relative to the chosen internship. Length of service: Teams range from six to eleven weeks.	Internship Teams include Agriculture, Art, Business, Education, International Affairs, Journalism, Medical Ministries, Social Work. Experienced workers with Youth With A Mission provide realistic international missions training pertinent to to the student's college major. COST—$1500 for six-week program plus airfare.

Name/Address Contact Person	Background of Agency	1991 Short-term Fields	Training Provided
The Fold Family Ministries P.O. Box 1188 Lyndonville, VT 05851 Fred Tomaselli Exec. Director	A residential, Christ-centered, discipleship ministry for teens, ages 13–17. Working with the whole family through counseling and training. The goals are evangelism, discipleship, and reconciliation of families.	Lyndonville, Vermont	Weekly staff training provided, including Christ-centered counseling and recommended reading.
Food for the Hungry 7729 E. Greenway Rd. Scottsdale, AZ 85260 800-248-6437 Lynn Morrill	Initiated in 1979, FH sends volunteers to over 14 countries to share their faith and skills through community development work. Also have an evangelistic program in Japan teaching English.	Kenya, Chad, Mozambique, Ethiopia, Laos, Thailand, Peru, Bolivia, Dom. Rep., Guatemala, Japan	Pre-field: 10 days for Japan candidates; 6 weeks for Third World positions. On field: orientation, language training, on-the-job training determined by Country Director.
Frontiers Mobilization Dept. P.O. Box 40159 Pasadena, CA 91114-7159 800-462-8436 = 800-GO-2-THEM	Frontiers is an innovative mission agency dedicated to raising up churches of Muslim converts throughout North Africa, the Middle East, and Asia. Distinctives: sole focus is Muslims, team organized and field-led, primary purpose is church-planting; on-field coaching, and grace-orientation.	Egypt, Turkey, Syria, Kazakhstan, Soviet Central Asia, Bangladesh, Indonesia and more	Duration varies from 2 to 11 weeks.
Global Outreach Mission P.O. Box 711 Buffalo, NY 14240 716-842-2220 Bill James	Begun in 1943, our main ministry is evangelism through many methods. "Fulfill your calling under our Umbrella." This gives the individual freedom to fulfill his calling in the ministry of his choice: summer, short-term, and career.	Europe, South America	Orientation for 4 days before leaving and as necessary on the field.
Gospel for Asia 1932 Walnut Plaza Carrollton, TX 75006 800-537-5357 Kris Davis	Gospel for Asia supports over 5,000 national missionaries in 10 Asian countries committed to evangelism and church planting. GFA's home office serves as an administrative link between the missionaries in the East and their sponsors in the West.	Carrollton, Texas or the hometown of Volunteer Area representatives	On-the-job training: instructors and materials to help develop personal support team.
Gospel Mission of South America, Inc. 1401 SW 21st Avenue Ft. Lauderdale, FL 33312 305-587-2975 Hudson Shedd	GMSA has the goal of establishing the local church.	Argentina, Chile & Uruguay	Arrive the first day of June; several days of orientation.
Gospel Missionary Union 10,000 North Oak Kansas City, MO 64155 816-734-8500 Rex Sandiford Candidate Director	GMU is an evangelical mission working in 20 countries. Many types of ministries are used to reach our objectives of evangelism, church planting and leadership training.	3 countries in: Latin America, Europe, Africa and Alaska	On-field orientation provided.
Greater Europe Mission P.O. Box 688 Wheaton, IL 60189 708-462-8050 Lowell Benson	GEM's goal is to train Europeans to evangelize greater Europe through their 10 Bible institutes, 3 seminaries and church-planting ministries scattered throughout Western Europe.	Austria, France, Belgium, Ireland, Spain, Portugal, E. Europe	Pre-field: two days of orientation. Field: length of orientation determined by missionary.

Appendix C: Short-term Mission Opportunities

Requirements/ Length of Service	Work Description and Cost
Love the Lord Jesus, love kids, desire to be a servant, and have a teachable spirit. Minimum 1 year commitment to serve (excluding internships and summer staff).	Personal evangelism and discipleship training opportunities with teens who want and need help. Live-in position affords opportunities for Christ-centered counseling to damaged and rejected teens. Rural Vermont farm setting.
Christians with heart to learn and to serve. Japan: College degree; Third World: technical degree. Length of service: 2 yrs for Japan, 3 yrs for Third World.	Japan: Evangelism through teaching conversational English classes, will raise $400/mo. for 2 yr term. Third World: Christian outreach and community development work in field of expertise, will raise $950/mo for 3 yr term.
Participants will spend their summer learning to befriend Muslims, overcome cultural barriers, and share Christ sensitively through language learning, living with Muslims and immersion in Muslim culture.	Discernment and spiritual warfare against cultural and religious strongholds of the enemy will be stressed. There are possibilities of musical involvement for some teams. Emphasis is on exposure to Muslim culture and church-planting issues, especially designed for those considering long-term commitment to God's Kingdom in the Muslim world. COST—varies from $1,400 to $2,600.
1 year of college for summer workers: Bible college suggested for short-term and career. All applicants considered as qualifications may differ with ministry. Summer 7–8 weeks; short term 1–3 yrs.	Summer ministry: evangelism teams, music, drama, children's meetings, open air, literature distribution, friendship evangelism, coffee house ministry. Summer cost $1,895. Short term: church planting, camping, radio, many types of evangelism.
1) Servant's heart and teachability. 2) Application and references. 3) Typing, computer data entry, writing, graphic arts, and/or the ability to communicate effectively highly desired. 4) 1 to 2 year commitment.	General office work and/or other duties depending on skills. COST—depends on need. Home office staff must raise their own support.
1) At least one year of Bible College or Institute. 2) Agreement to the doctrinal statement. 3) Four references including pastor's. 4) A teachable spirit. Work 8 weeks of the summer.	Opportunities to minister, have classes, help in construction and see the work as a whole. From Miami to either Santiago de Chile or Buenos Aires, round trip approximately $750, plus $200 per month towards board and room.
1) Must be a Christian. 2) Completed at least one year of college. 3) Application procedure. Summer: 2–10 weeks, Short term: 1–2 years.	Camp ministries, evangelism, VBS, construction, maintenance. Muslim ministries, campaigns, secretarial, team ministries, music outreach. COST—transportation plus $2–11 per day, depending on country.
1) At least 1 year of college. 2) Agreement with doctrinal statement. 3) Application and medical forms. 4) Five references including pastor's. 5) Willing to work hard and serve others. Length: summer–8 weeks.	Evangelism teams: door-to-door work, surveys, street meetings. Music teams: concerts in churches, shopping centers and special meetings. Maintenance teams: construction, painting, cleaning, kitchen work, clerical work, etc. COST—$2775 for entire summer.

Name/Address Contact Person	Background of Agency	1991 Short-term Fields	Training Provided
HCJB World Radio P.O. Box 553000 Opa Locka, FL 33055 305-624-4252 Mr. Ed Giesbrecht	HCJB uses international and local broadcasting, health care, training and evangelism to proclaim the gospel and disciple believers, especially in unreached and under-reached regions.	Ecuador, Texas, Indiana, Miami	College-age summer workers assisted in orientation. All opportunities require some level of specific education and experience.
Harvesting in Spanish 245 S. Benton St. #100 Denver, CO 80226-2422 Don Brenner	Begun in 1980, H.I.S. has had phenomenal growth in Spanish-speaking countries, with many missionaries serving in numerous people groups worldwide.	El Salvador and Guatemala	Very little formal training.
Hellenic Missionary Union Project Mars Hill Lydias 12 115 27 Athens, Greece (011) 301-777-9845	Ministering in Greece since 1980 through widespread evangelism, church planting, and promotion of world missions.	Greece	See Work Description.
InterAct Ministries 31000 SE Kelson Rd. Boring, OR 97009 503-668-5571 Jerry Crosby	Since its inception in 1951 InterAct Ministries has been committed to reaching the unreached people of North America through cross-cultural evangelism, discipleship and church planting.	USA and Canada	Summer Impact: One-week pre-field orientation as well as continuing training and evaluation throughout the 8-week program. Short Term: training in cross-cultural communication, evangelism strategies, etc. on-site.
International Missions Network Center Box 7 Elm Springs, AR 72728 501-248-7236 Fax 501-248-1455	The International Missions Network Center was founded in 1975 by Oren Paris, and serves the growing network of ministries worldwide. The IMNC is currently home to 12 major ministries, including Youth With A Mission-Elim Springs, Bibles for the Nations, Word for the World, Living Alternatives, and many others.	USSR, Poland, Hungary, Yugoslavia, Africa, Jamaica, Asia, Central America, Brazil, Mexico, inner-city USA	Pre-field orientation and any necessary training are provided. For longer terms of service, Discipleship Training Schools and other specialized schools and programs are available.
International Teams P.O. Box 203 Prospect Heights, IL 60070 800-323-0428 Glen Schuman	An evangelical, non-denominational missions agency, training and sending teams of two-year missionaries overseas since 1961. These teams prepare at training center for five months. Summer and career options available.	Western Europe, Greece, Poland, Czechoslovakia, Hungary, Romania, Bulgaria, Soviet Union, Philippines, Urban USA, Canada	Pre-field: 4 days, summer terms; 5 months, 2-yr. teams. Language, culture, interpersonal relations, evangelism, discipleship. On-field: On-the-job with experienced missionaries and further language.
International Union of Gospel Missions P.O. Box 10780 Kansas City, MO 64118 800-624-5156 Michael Limatta	Begun in 1971, the IUGM is an association of rescue missions serving Christ in the inner cities of the U.S., Canada, and overseas.	United States and Canada	Each mission provides training that is appropriate to the positions available in their local ministry.
Latin America Mission/Spearhead P.O. Box 52-7900 Miami, FL 33152 305-884-8400 Donna Johnson	LAM works throughout Latin America, evangelizing, discipling, helping the needy. The Spearhead program is designed to give young adults meaningful service experience and in-depth exposure to another culture.	Mexico City, Central America	On-the-field orientation, language and cross-cultural classes.

Appendix C: Short-term Mission Opportunities

Requirements/Length of Service	Work Description and Cost
At least two years of college for 9-week summer program; other areas have differing requirements based on position. Short-term service: 2 weeks to three months; full-time: three years and special assignments.	COST—Summer program approx. $2,000. Other short-term workers raise support based on field and length of service.
2 weeks to 2 years service preferred for short term missionaries. Teams for 10 days to 2 weeks: Christians of age 16 and up with a pastor's reference can apply.	Caring for children, ministering on streets and in markets, construction activities, orphanage work. COST—ranges from $5 to $25 per day, plus air fare, depending on country and project.
Summer program: See Work Description for full detail. Year-round opportunities: Building, mechanical, and secretarial skills needed.	Project Mars Hill summer program: Multi-faceted exposure to missions in Greece through informative seminars and interviews of Christian leaders, cultural exposure, involvement in the annual Greek Missions Conference, work project, participation in HMU's Evangelistic Campaign throughout Greece, visits to historical sites, and development of international working abilities.
One year of college or Bible school, satisfactory references, agreement with InterAct doctrinal statement. Summer Impact is 8 weeks, Short Term is 1 to 2 years.	1) Friendship evangelism and discipleship in a cross-cultural setting, or 2) Youth camping. Cost for Summer Impact is $50–$750 depending on program chosen. Short Term monthly support required is $950 for singles, $1650 for couples.
Outreaches normally 1 to 3 weeks. Short and long term service available.	Bible distribution, mercy ministry, construction, door-to-door and street evangelism are combined with other forms of ministry to provide unique opportunities in each outreach location. Outreaches reach throughout the world. Costs vary.
1) Personal faith in Christ. 2) Summer: Minimum age 18; 2-yrs: Minimum age 20. Length of service: 1 month or 2 years (plus training).	Personal evangelism, discipleship, church planting, open-air meetings, drama, music, puppets, children's meetings, films, literature distribution, TESL, community development (Philippines urban poor). COST—2 yr: $1,100–1,350/mo.; Summer: $2,050–2,250.
1) Personal relationship with Christ. 2) Heart for the people of the inner city. 3) At least 18 years old. 4) One year out of high school, preferred. Summer opportunities and one year Leadership Training Program are available.	Most summer opportunities involve working with urban youth in inner city outreach and camping programs. Positions with family shelters, rehabilitation programs, and other social welfare and evangelistic outreaches are also available. Most summer positions are paid, with some volunteer opportunities.
1) Personal relationship with Jesus; desire to serve Him in another culture. 2) 19–30 years old. 3) Some Spanish language background helpful. Length of service: Summer, 1 or 2 years.	Neighborhood evangelism, literature distribution, youth rallies, work with inner-city gangs, music and drama outreach in parks, markets and prisons. Volunteers live with Latin families. Unusual opportunity to penetrate Latin culture. COST—$695 for summer (June-August), $500 per month for one year or more.

Name/Address Contact Person	Background of Agency	1991 Short- term Fields	Training Provided
Liebenzell Mission Intl. U.S.: Scholey's Mtn., NJ 07870 Canada: Moffat, Ontario, L0P 1J0 908-852-3044 Juanita Simpson	Liebenzell, an evangelical, interdenominational faith mission, is committed to the proclamation of the Gospel, and the nurturing of the believer, wherever God may lead.	Micronesia, Melanesia, Japan, Burundi, others	Pre-field: Two-week orientation at Headquarters. Field: length determined by field director.
Life Investment A Division of Kingdom Building Ministries 4221 S. Harmon St. Marion, IN 46953 317-674-2448 Steve Moore	Evangelical, non-denominational ministry, training and sending teams of young adults on short-term evangelism projects. The goal of Life Investment is to provide participants with hands-on cross-cultural ministry experience and develop World Christian commitment.	Bolivia, Nicaragua, Romania/Russia, India, Denver, CO, Inner City	2–4 day Life Investment Training Conference.
LIFE Ministries P.O. Box 200 San Dimas, CA 91773 800-272-5433 or 714-599-8491 Rob Honcoop	Founded as a short-term ministry committed to the training and growth of its missionaries and to facilitating effective ministry in the church in Japan—LIFE is committed to building partnerships between North American and Japanese churches.	Japan: Staff Needed: Summer, 112; One-yr., 27; 2 1/2 to 3 yrs., 30.	Pre-field: 2 to 4 day orientation. Field: 2 to 3 week initial, as well as ongoing, training in evangelism, and the culture and language of Japan. Re-entry: 2 to 3 day debriefing.
Mercy Ships P.O. Box 2020 Lindale, TX 75771 800-772-SHIP Personnel Office	The M/V Anastasis and the M/V Good Samaritan sail to needy countries with medical services and practical aid for physical needs, and a gospel message of eternal hope.	Sail between Africa and Europe; U.S. and the Caribbean Basin.	No mission training is required for short-term workers. Pre-departure info pack. Orientation provided on-board. Discipleship training school is available for long-term workers.
Mexican Medical, Inc. 13901 Lyons Valley Rd., Ste C Jamul, CA 91935 619-669-0608 Mel Peabody, Ph.D.	MexMed's goal is to serve the people of Mexico by providing physical healing through medicine and spiritual healing through the gospel of Jesus Christ. Nine medical facilities throughout Mexico.	Mexico: Chiapas, Baltibiltic, Morelia, San Quintin, Tijuana, San Felipe	Training manual and two-day orientation, on-the-job training.
Mexico Summer Training Session 4517-A Broadmoor Ave. Grand Rapids, MI 49512 616-698-8393 Dr. Dick L. Van Halsema	Mexico STS, sponsored by I.D.E.A. Ministries, since 1968 has provided academic-practical preparation for cross-cultural ministry in all parts of the world.	Mexico, Belize and Honduras	Advance readings. During STS, 3 semester credit courses: History of Mexico, Spanish, field work—plus Bible study, mission classes.
Middle East Training Session 4517-A Broadmoor Ave. Grand Rapids, MI 49512 616-698-8393 Dr. Dick L. Van Halsema	METS 1991, sponsored by I.D.E.A. Ministries, provides academic and practical preparation for Christian service in Muslim context; begun in 1979.	Egypt (optional travel to nearby countries, extra cost)	Advance readings. METS includes intensive Islamics course near Cairo, plus 4 weeks of practical assignment—plus Bible studies, lectures on culture, history.
Missionary World Service and Evangelism P.O. Box 123 Wilmore, KY 40390-0123 606-858-3171 C. V. Elliott	MWS&E works in partnership with foreign mission agencies and indigenous ministries in numerous countries, assisting in construction, service projects, witnessing, and preaching. We channel gifts to overseas programs.	American Indian, Brazil, Paraguay, Mexico, India, Kenya	Advance information and orientation on day of departure.

Appendix C: Short-term Mission Opportunities

Requirements/Length of Service	Work Description and Cost
A personal faith in Christ, and a strong commitment to His Great Commission. Bible and other training according to the position. Two years service.	Evangelism, Discipleship, Christian Education, Christian Teachers, Pastoral Training, TEE, Literature Outreach, Youth Work, Community Health Trainers. Costs vary greatly according to location: $900+ per month.
Committed to Christ and at least 17 years of age. Length of service: 1 week to 1 month.	Teams primarily involved in evangelistic activities. Use a variety of ministry tools such as music, drama, personal testimony, and literature distribution. Ministry in churches, parks, public squares, schools, prisons, films and concerts. COST—varies according to air fare and in-country expenses—usually between $500 and $2,500.
Summer: 19 years of age or 1 yr college. One to three years: (leaving March or September of each year) 21 years of age, healthy, flexible attitude, high motivation.	Teamed with Japanese Christians to minister in church planting and church growth through teaching conversational English and leading Bible studies. Involved in chapels and evangelistic camps. Focused on friendship evangelism and "building bridges" between your students and church members. Secretary and support personnel also vitally needed. COST—varies according to ministry.
Committed Christians with positive references, in good health, at least 18 years old. Invited to apply for 2 weeks to 3 month term.	Surgical/primary health care opportunities for medical professionals. Workers needed for deck crew, galley, hospitality, clerical, engine room, electrical, plumbing, child care, construction. Evangelism opportunities for all. COST—Volunteers pay trans. costs to and from ship. Crew fees (inc. room and board): $150/mo.
Formal or lay biblical training. Personal faith in Jesus Christ. Spanish preferred. Service: 1 week to 2 years.	Minister in medicine, evangelism and other work projects. Evangelism: door-to-door, vacation Bible school, film ministries. Working with local churches. COST—2 yr: based on individual need; 9 wks summer: $500.
High school graduation 1990 or before. Church appointment, good health, prayer support. 8-1/2 weeks: June 15-Aug. 14 (extended field work available, 4-12 mos.).	Personal and team evangelism, vacation Bible school teams, service with national churches and missions. $25 registration, $850 program (plus travel, expenses)....
Year of college completed. 2.2 GPA min. Church appointment, good health, prayer support. 7 weeks: May 27 to July 15 (extended stay may be possible).	Academic study, field trips, practical assignments with national churches or agencies. $25 registration, $995 subsidized program cost plus travel, expenses....
People from any Christian background age 16 or older, who desire to serve and grow in a cross-cultural setting. Length of service: 10 days to 3 weeks.	Variety of work and service projects plus opportunities for witness and fellowship in other cultural settings. Costs vary according to field of service.

Name/Address Contact Person	Background of Agency	1991 Short- term Fields	Training Provided
Missions Outreach International P.O. Box 73 Bethany, MO 64424 800-543-9732 Teen Ministries Coordinator	Purpose is to provide exposure and practical ministry training for high school & college students overseas. This is done through summer opportunities in which students work with well-established mission boards.	Belize, Costa Rica, Guatemala, Peru, Zambia, Fiji, Bolivia, Indonesia, Ireland	5 days of training are provided. Evangelism, construction, and basic cross-cultural communication skills are all included as well as regular times of Bible study.
N.E.W. Missions P.O. Box 2880 Worcester, MA 01613 508-752-7352 George DeTellis	Established in 1983, diversified mission to the country of Haiti, 13 churches established, feeding and educating 3,000 plus children. High School and Bible College with a projected attendance of over 1,000 students. Full-scale medical facilities.	Haiti	Pre-departure training is done by way of video, cassette tapes, and team meetings prior to departure.
OC STEP 25 Corning Ave. Milpitas, CA 95035 800-676-STEP	OC International (Overseas Crusades, established in 1950, serves in 17 countries). Its objective of reaching the whole nation for Christ is to be achieved through the motivation, training, and mobilization of local churches.	Mexico City, Philippines, Zimbabwe	Various types of training provided.
OMS International P.O. Box A Greenwood, IN 46142 317-881-6751 Julia Hunt	Formerly the Oriental Missionary Society, founded in 1901 by Chicago telegrapher Charles Cowman and wife Lettie, author of *Streams in the Desert*. Its primary emphasis ever since has been evangelism, church planting, theological education.	S. Amer., France, Spain, H. Kong, India, Indonesia, Japan, Korea, Taiwan, & U.S.	Training manual with "To Do" checklists to be accomplished before departure. 24-hour port-of-departure orientation, specific in-country training upon arrival.
Operation Mobilization P.O. Box 2277 Peachtree City, GA 30269 404-631-0432 Keith Haywood	OM began in 1957 in Mexico and spread into Europe. In the 60's teams moved out to the Middle East and South Asia. In the 70's the Logos and Doulos ship ministry was launched.	Europe, Middle East, Asia, Mexico, Quebec, and ships Logos II and Doulos	Orientation materials, conferences, hands-on experience, training in personal discipleship, interpersonal relationships and cross-cultural evangelism.
Overseas Missionary Fellowship 404 South Church Street Robesonia, PA 19551 215-693-5681 Brenda Steadman	Founded as the China Inland Mission in 1865, OMF's goal is an active church in every Asian community, with a particular focus on neglected or unreached people groups in Asia.	Japan, Indonesia, the Philippines, Hong Kong, Taiwan, USA plus an educational exchange in China	Several days of formal, pre-field training for Japan and China are done upon arrival. Each short-term worker will be provided with a travel manual and orientation handbook for their particular field.
Partners International 1470 N. Fourth Street P.O. Box 15025 San Jose, CA 95112 408-453-3800 Don Maselli	Since 1943, Partners International has assisted national Christians in ministering to their countrymen. The emphasis of this interdenominational ministry is to assist national evangelists and church planters.	Brazil, Guatemala, Mexico, India, Indonesia, Philippines, Kenya, Nigeria, Zambia, Belgium, Yugoslavia	Write for details.

Appendix C: Short-term Mission Opportunities

Requirements/ Length of Service	Work Description and Cost
A growing Christian who desires to be stretched; prepared to live without many of the comforts of home and in a team setting with people who come from wide backgrounds of Christian faith.	The exposure and training includes specified work projects as well as opportunities for evangelism and worship in other cultural contexts. COST—varies with length and field of service: $1,200–$3,000.
One week to 3 month short-term mission service.	Evangelism by way of crusades and working with mission churches. Construction projects. Medical teams with specialized projects servicing the mission school children and regional village populations.. COST—$200 per week, $500 per month, includes food, lodging, and transportation in the country of Haiti.
At least 18 years of age, a Christian for at least 2 years, experience in Christian service, a servant's heart. Length of service: 8 weeks. Spanish-speaking required for Mexico.	In the context of a local church, with at least one U.S. partner, assist local volunteers to engage in models of ministry proven effective in that community. Models include evangelistic, home Bible studies, discipleship groups, vacation Bible school. COST—$1,400–3,000 depending on country.
1) Christian with teachable spirit. 2) College or one year out of high school. 3) Flexible attitude. Length of service: 2-5 months. Fall assignments available. Summer most popular.	Program varies with the country. English evangelism priority in Orient. Assist the missionaries however possible. Involvement with National Christians. Foreign language not required. Could involve some maintenance or secretarial depending on your skills. COST—$1,700–3,200 depending on field.
17 years of age or older, have been a Christian for at least 1 year, be recommended by their church and come with an attitude to learn, grow and serve. Length of service: Summer-2 to 6 wks, 1 to 2 years.	Summer teams major in evangelism. Methods include friendship evangelism, street meetings using music, drama, sketchboard; visiting homes, coffee bars; film/video. One/two year programs include evangelistic teams, support teams, maintaining ships, etc. COST—$500 per month, 1 & 2 years; $1600–2200 for summer.
1) Know Christ as Savior and Lord. 2) At least a freshman in college, 18 or older. 3) Display evident spiritual maturity (acceptable references). 4) Be in good health. Length of service: 6 week minimum.	Japan: teach English for evangelism. China: study Mandarin and Asian culture or teach (professionals only). Other fields: evangelism, English classes, camps, Bible studies, literature sales, construction, maintenance, refugee work & mobilization. COST—$1,500–$3,300. Airfare to Asia included and subject to change.
A heart to serve the Lord by empowering nationals, a mind open to and accepting of cultural differences, proficiency and confidence in your field of expertise. Some college or work experience is preferred.	There is a great variety of needs within our partner ministries, including work teams, summer youth workers, and professionals who can teach their specialty. COST—$1200–$2000 for summer work teams, and $1000-$2000 per month for longer assignments.

Name/Address Contact Person	Background of Agency	1991 Short-term Fields	Training Provided
Royal Servants International 5517 Warwick Place Minneapolis, MN 55436 612-925-3519 Louis Inks	RSI's goal is to EXPOSE students to the world's burning need for a Savior; EQUIP them to help meet that need through discipleship; and SEND them back home to be actively involved in ministry. RSI has been sending teams to Europe every summer since 1981.	Austria, Belgium, Czechoslovakia, England, France, Germany, Italy, the Netherlands, Poland, Scotland, Spain, Switzerland	A two-week training period is provided to help students develop ministry skills as well as learn how to share their faith.
SEND International P.O. Box 513 Farmington, MI 48332 313-477-4210 Verona Dutton	SEND is an evangelical, interdenominational mission with ministry in Alaska, Japan, the Philippines, Taiwan, Spain, Eastern Europe, Russia and Hong Kong. The main focus is on church planting.	Alaska, Japan, Taiwan, Philippines, Spain, Hong Kong	Pre-field: Required reading. On-field: 1-2 weeks of orientation.
SIM USA Box 7900 Charlotte, NC 28241 704-588-4300 Ken Lloyd or Les Unruh	Since 1893, SIM has been taking the gospel to unreached peoples, teaching the Word, planting churches, restoring the sick to health, feeding the hungry, and building new circles of believers for the Lord. Over 7,000 congregations have come into being through SIM's diverse ministry. Over two million people have come to know Christ.	Bangladesh, Benin, Bolivia, Burkina Faso, Chile, Cote d'Ivoire, Ecuador, Ethiopia, Ghana, Guinea, India, Kenya, Liberia, Niger, Nigeria, Pakistan, Peru, others	Two days to three weeks of pre-field presentation on how to cope with culture shock, interpersonal relationships, travel arrangements, and God's perspective on missions.
SIMA Mission to the World P.O. Box 29765 Atlanta, GA 30359 404-320-3373	Evangelical mission of the Presbyterian Church in America founded in 1974; career options available; "Go for a Season and Still Reap the Harvest."	28 countries: Africa, Asia, Australia, Europe, Caribbean, Latin America	Depends on program: cross-cultural preparation and support-raising for all; language training for 2 year; pre-field training and on-site orientation for 2 month; training manual and project orientation with leadership training for 2 week.
STEM Ministries P.O. Box 290066 Minneapolis, MN 55249 612-535-2944 Team Operations: Janet, Pat, Kitty	STEM (Short Term Evangelical Missions Ministries) organizes teams of laypeople from churches and fellowships across the nation as 2-week "short-term" missionaries to work with national pastors and Christian workers in the Caribbean.	Haiti, Trinidad, Jamaica 300–500 volunteers	Team Training Manual and 4-8 hours of pre-field preparation. Additional on-location training of 8 hours specifically geared toward the work. Debriefing prior to return home.
South America Mission P.O. Box 6560 Lake Worth, FL 33466 407-965-1833 Lori Stobbe	Began in Brazil in 1914. Emphasis on church planting, evangelism and discipleship. Service ministries include aviation, work among the handicapped, teaching M.K.s.	Bolivia, Brazil, Colombia and Peru	Summer teams: 1-2 day orientation and debriefing. Short terms: 2 week candidate school.
Training and Service Corps 4517-A Broadmoor Ave. Grand Rapids, MI 49512-5339 616-698-8393 Dr. Dick L. Van Halsema	TASC is sponsored by I.D.E.A. Ministries. Provides 2 or 2 1/2 year study and service for college graduates, teams of 2 per each.	Mexico and Turkey primarily. Other countries have received teams also.	Candidate Semester at Reformed Bible College, language study abroad, supervised field service.

Appendix C: Short-term Mission Opportunities

Requirements/ Length of Service	Work Description and Cost
Christians age 13 and over with church approval. Length: Summer–8 weeks.	Personal evangelism and intense discipleship. Students learn to share the Gospel using music, drama, puppets and clowning. COST—$2,800.
1) Personal faith in Jesus Christ, a desire to serve Him, and an ability to share faith. 2) Two years post-high school. 3) Application process and good health. Length of service: Summer (10 weeks).	Asia: Evangelism, TESL, camping, discipleship training. Alaska: Village ministries, camping, nursing, secretarial, radio and maintenance. COST—$625–$1,500 and airfare.
Adult believers who want to spread the Word to people in the developing countries of Africa, Asia, and South America. Lengths of service can vary from one month to one year. Opportunities are also available for church/youth groups to serve in a team ministry.	Business and administration, development, education, theological education, evangelism, media, health, technical services. COST—$2,285–$3,235.
2 years: age 21 up, college grad or necessary experience, should be familiar with Westminster Confession of Faith, raise own funds. *2 months*: age 18 up, or one year of college, should be familiar with Westminster Confession of Faith, raise own funds. *2 weeks*: junior or senior high student, or adult.	Evangelism, discipleship, church planting, English instruction, teaching, children's ministry, church nurture, construction. COST—2 years: $1,500–3000/month; 2 months: $1,500–3500; 2 weeks: $500–1000.
All ages: willing hearts and hands, confession of faith. Teams available throughout the entire calendar year. Individuals or groups may join or form a team. Length of service: 2 weeks. (Longer terms also available.)	Each STEM will share in evangelism, various construction, mercy/service/creative ministries. In all situations, STEM works with you and your church here at home in order to help the local church overseas grow and multiply. COST—Averages $1000 (includes airfare).
Summer Teams: 1 year college, 1 and 2 month programs. Short terms: Requirements vary, 1–3 yr. service. Work teams: Requirements vary, 1–3 weeks service.	Opportunities include personal evangelism, discipleship, exposure to church planting, teaching, medical work and construction (work teams). COST—Summer teams: $1,640 to $2,090; Short terms: monthly support must be raised; Work teams: costs vary.
Completion of Mexico STS or METS (see listings), church appointments. 2 or 2 1/2 year program depending on language study duration. Begin any Jan., June, or Sept.	Main goal of TASC: after Candidate Semester and language study, 12-month minimum of supervised ministry, often with supplemental service (e.g., teaching English, social work, nursing, etc.).

Name/Address Contact Person	Background of Agency	1991 Short- term Fields	Training Provided
United World Mission P.O. Box 250 Union Mills, NC 28167 704-287-8996 800-INTO-UWM Betty Sadler	Founded in 1946, UWM is committed to saturating peoples and geographical areas with local churches through the proclamation of demonstration of the Gospel of Jesus Christ.	Europe, Africa, Latin America, India	2–8 weeks: 1–3 days pre-field plus on-field orientation. Two years: 4 weeks pre-field training; language study may be required.
University Language Services P.O. Box 701984 Tulsa, OK 74170 918-495-7045 Dick Gaffney	ULS's goal is to provide excellent teaching in the classroom, to establish friendships and to provide information about God's love for the Chinese people.	China	3 weeks orientation beginning Aug. 1. Includes training in teaching Eng. as a second lang., culture, Chinese as lang., how to witness.
Venture Teams International P.O. Box 186, Sub. 158 Calgary, Alberta 403-291-3725 Len Lane	Began in 1979 in Calgary, Alberta. Founded by Rev. Mel Slack, a former missionary to India. Interdenominational and inter-mission.	Africa, Australia/ Indonesia, Eastern Europe, Caribbean, Brazil, Pakistan, Philippines, Taiwan, Japan	7 weeks pre-field training, cross-cultural, some language if necessary. Perspectives on the World Christian Movement course.
World Gospel Mission Box 948 Marion, IN 49652-0948 317-664-7331	World Gospel Mission is an interdenominational missionary sending organization with approximately 350 missionaries and homeland staff serving on five continents. Founded in 1910, WGM is thoroughly evangelistic and dedicated to leading men, women, and children to a full and personal knowledge of our Lord and Savior, Jesus Christ.	American Indian, American Inner-Cities, Argentina, Bolivia, Haiti, Honduras, India, Japan, Kenya, Mexico, Paraguay, Spain, Taiwan, Tanzania	Varies according to position.
World Servants 8233 Gator Lane, #6 West Palm Beach, FL 33411 407-790-0800 Maury Buchanan	World Servants is uniquely designed to coordinate mission efforts of local churches throughout the world. This year over 1800 people participated in World Servants projects, building churches, schools and homes and sharing the message of Christ.	Bolivia, Brazil, Dominican Rep., Ecuador, Egypt, Hungary, Jamaica, Kenya, Mexico, Puerto Rico, U.S.	Pre-field orientation provided for leaders of each group, 3 to 4 days in length.
Wycliffe Bible Translators P.O. Box 2727 Huntington Beach, CA 92647 714-969-4600 800-338-1928 Richard Whitmire	The Wycliffe team's primary goal is to provide God's Word to over 300 million people without the Bible. Short-term workers continue to meet critical personnel needs.	Africa, Asia, Latin America, North America, Pacific	Varies according to position.
Youth for Christ P.O. Box 228822 Denver, CO 80222 303-843-9000 Larry Williams	YFC is a non-denominational ministry that has been reaching young people around the world with the gospel since 1944.	South Africa, Mexico, Jamaica, Dominican Republic, Honduras, Ghana, Kenya, others	2 day orientation for 2 week trips; 2 1/2 months on field training for 10 month ministry teams.

Appendix C: Short-term Mission Opportunities

Requirements/ Length of Service	Work Description and Cost
2-8 weeks: growing Christians with teachable spirit, needed skills. Two years: education and/or experience for the assignment.	2-8 weeks: builders teams; children's/youth outreach, neighborhood evangelism with local churches; vocational skills; $1500–2500. Two years: MK staff, evangelism/discipleship, agricultural/community development, medical, leadership training. Monthly support requirement varies according to country.
1) Bachelor's degree. 2) Application with and acceptance from ULS. 3) Call to China. 1 yr contract minimum long term; Summer. term 4 wks.	Teaching English in Chinese colleges and universities. Establishing friendships and witnessing as the opportunity arises. No open evangelism. Salary, housing, medical care provided by host. COST—approx. $4500 for training/placement/transportation.
19 years of age or older, Bible knowledge, flexibility, maturity, personal faith in Christ, music/drama or church planting skills. 1 or 2 years duration.	Two types of teams: music/drama or church planting. Minimum of 4 months cross-cultural experience. Emphasis on evangelism. Cost: dependent upon geographical location.
Desire to serve the Lord and help others.	*Teams* work shoulder to shoulder with missionaries and national Christians on a building or maintenance project and minister in area churches through music and testimonies. 10 days–2 weeks. High school, college, adult. *Individuals* searching God's will and wanting to minister—6 weeks–2 years. College and young career. COST—range: $500–$2,700.
Willingness to learn, serve and tell the story of what Christ has done in your life.	Construction, health care, door-to-door evangelism, community development, street evangelism and children's ministry. One to three week projects. COST—ranges from $345 to $1,370.
Ranges from four weeks to five years.	You can find a place of fulfillment on the Bible translation team. A wide range of opportunities are available like teachers, accountants, secretaries and computer programmers. COST—Varies with assignment.
High school and older for 2-3 week Project Serve Trips; out of high school for 10 month Harvest team ministry.	Project Serve teams participate in construction or renovation and minister in the local community; Cost: $300–$2400 depending on location. Harvest teams travel throughout South Africa, ministering in schools through music and drama; Cost: $9,000.

Name/Address Contact Person	Background of Agency	1991 Short-term Fields	Training Provided
Youth With A Mission P.O. Box 4600 Tyler, TX 75712 903-882-5591 Fax: 903-882-9297 Bill Heaps	Founded in 1960, YWAM mobilizes short- and long-term missions teams. Over 300 centers in 85 nations cooperate with local churches in EVANGELISM, TRAINING, and MERCY MINISTRY—practical assistance to those in need. YWAM Tyler, Texas offers a variety of training programs, and year-round short-term opportunities worldwide.	Nicaragua, Cuba, Mexico, Eastern Europe, Haiti, Costa Rica, Canada, U.S.	One to seven days of orientation and ministry preparation. The Discipleship Training School includes three months of training and two months of field work. The high school SST program involves two weeks of training and one week in Mexico.
Youth With A Mission-Maui P.O. Box 237 Paia-Maui, HI 96779 808-579-8402 Fax: 808-579-8405 Tom Bauer	Youth With A Mission-Maui provides short- and long-term opportunities for those interested in the South Pacific and Asia. Whether it is here in Maui or abroad, we can equip you with a project or a training school to help you set and attain ministry goals.	Micronesia, Fiji, Taiwan, India, Singapore, Philippines, Malaysia, Japan, Maui or Hawaii, Salt Lake City (Utah)	Short-term outreaches are preceded by a 2 week orientation. Discipleship Training Schools contain 3 month preparation phase. During this training the participant is challenged to know God and make Him known. "Go For It!"
Youth With A Mission-Utah P.O. Box 11953 Salt Lake City, UT 84147 801-399-3108 Jim Pitts	Youth With A Mission-Salt Lake City trains short- and long-term workers and specializes in working amongst people involved in the cults. Utah is probably the least evangelical state in America and the needs are great here.	Tonga, Utah, Alaska, Hawaii	We provide the training you need for each destination. Training periods vary. Shorter orientation time for short outreaches and a 3 month training period for our Discipleship Training School.

This material is reprinted by permission from *The Great Commission Handbook*, published by Berry Publishing Services, Inc. Copies may be ordered by writing or calling 701 Main Street, Evanston, IL 60202; 708/869-1573.

Appendix C: Short-term Mission Opportunities

Requirements/ Length of Service	Work Description and Cost
1) Submission to Christ. 2) Completion of application with medical forms and references. 3) Age requirements vary with location, program and type of ministry.	Short-term outreaches participate in: 1) EVANGELISM: literature distribution, personal evangelism, drama, music, children's ministry. 2) MERCY MINISTRY: construction, distribution of food and clothing, etc. COSTS—vary with location and length of participation.
Application with 2 references. Adventurous spirit and a willingness to learn. Take a risk! Short term outreaches 4–6 weeks; Volunteer Service 1 week to 3 months; Training schools are 5 months.	Costs vary according to destination and length of school. Each adventure offers varied Ministry opportunities including Open-Airs, Door to Door, Drama, Puppetry, Church planting, Service Projects and other Evangelistic activities.
Discipleship Training School. Commit yourself for one week or up to 5 months or even longer. We have a training opportunity to serve you depending on your availability. Whether you want to focus on Utah or another destination—near or far—we can facilitate you.	Here in Utah our main focus is toward Mormons. Write us for costs for specific training schools. Our outreaches target the many Mormon pageants and activities and also reach Native Americans in the area. Our ministry methods are varied—but always exciting!

APPENDIX D
Charts on Factors Impacting Family Life

PERCENT OF CHRISTIAN MONEY SPENT ON WORLD POPULATION

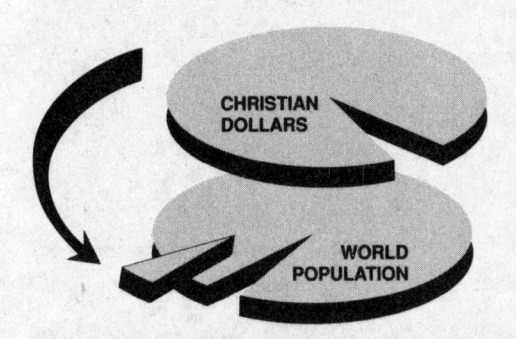

CHRISTIAN DOLLARS

WORLD POPULATION

96% OF ALL CHRISTIAN DOLLARS GO TO ONLY 6% OF THE WORLD'S POPULATION

EARLY DATING PROMOTES FORNICATION

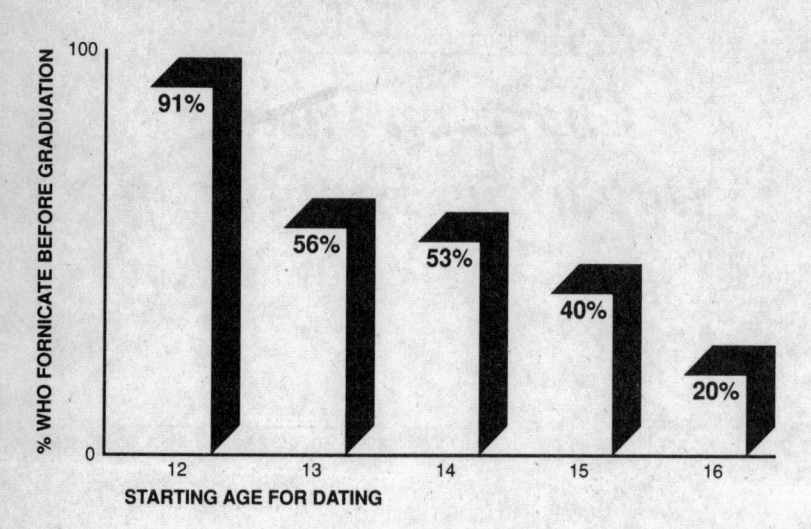

% WHO FORNICATE BEFORE GRADUATION

- Age 12: 91%
- Age 13: 56%
- Age 14: 53%
- Age 15: 40%
- Age 16: 20%

STARTING AGE FOR DATING

U.S. FERTILITY FREEFALL

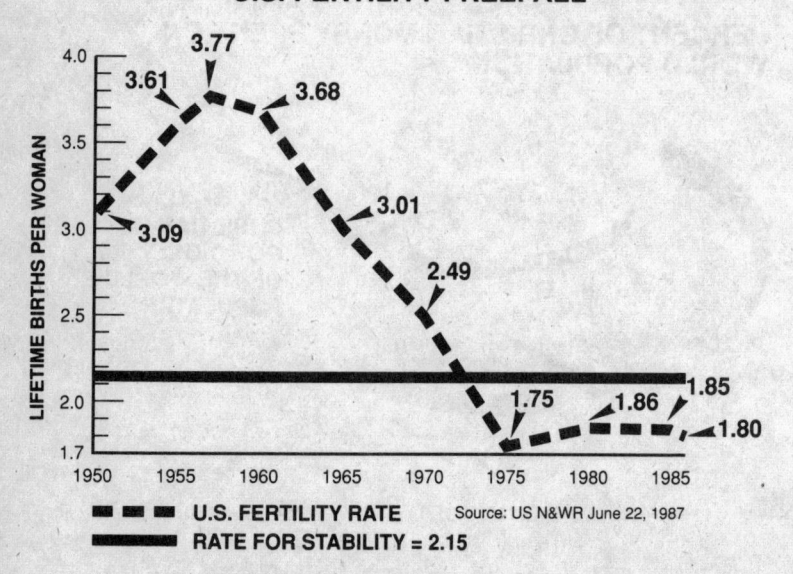

LIFETIME BIRTHS PER WOMAN

- 1950: 3.09
- 1955: 3.61
- (peak) 3.77
- 1960: 3.68
- 1965: 3.01
- 1970: 2.49
- 1975: 1.75
- 1980: 1.86
- 1985: 1.85
- 1.80

----- U.S. FERTILITY RATE
—— RATE FOR STABILITY = 2.15

Source: US N&WR June 22, 1987

Appendix D: Charts on Factors Impacting Family Life

LONG-RANGE PICTURE OF FERTILITY SLIDE

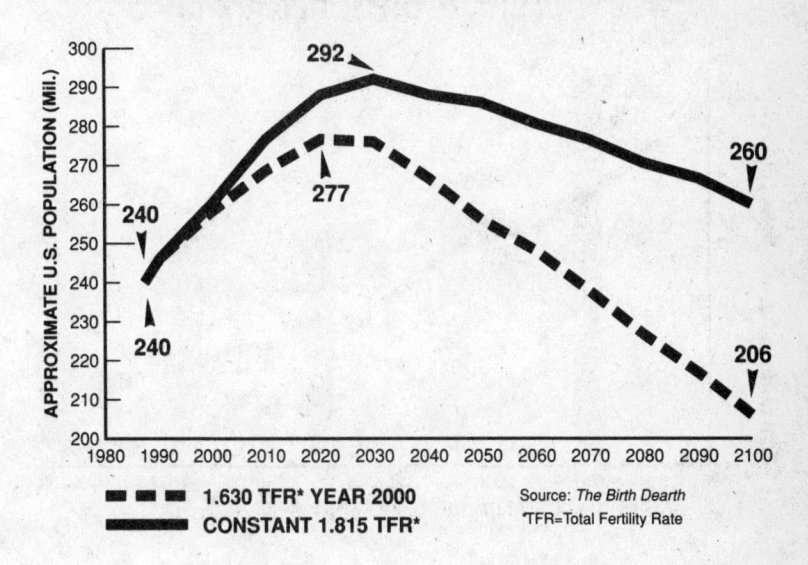

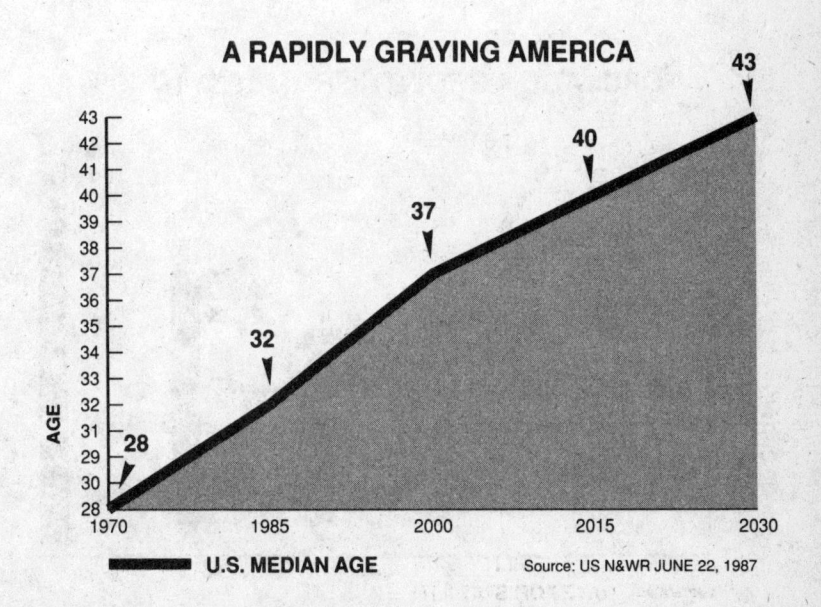

APPROXIMATE U.S. POPULATION (Mil.)

- - - 1.630 TFR* YEAR 2000
—— CONSTANT 1.815 TFR*

Source: *The Birth Dearth*
*TFR=Total Fertility Rate

A RAPIDLY GRAYING AMERICA

AGE

—— U.S. MEDIAN AGE

Source: US N&WR JUNE 22, 1987

WESTERN SHARE OF WORLD POPULATION

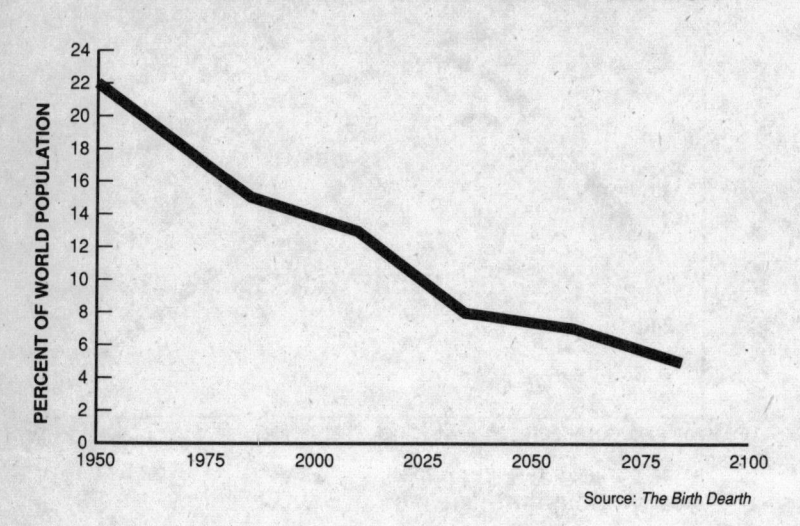

Source: The Birth Dearth

POPULATION GROWTH FROM 1934 TO 1984

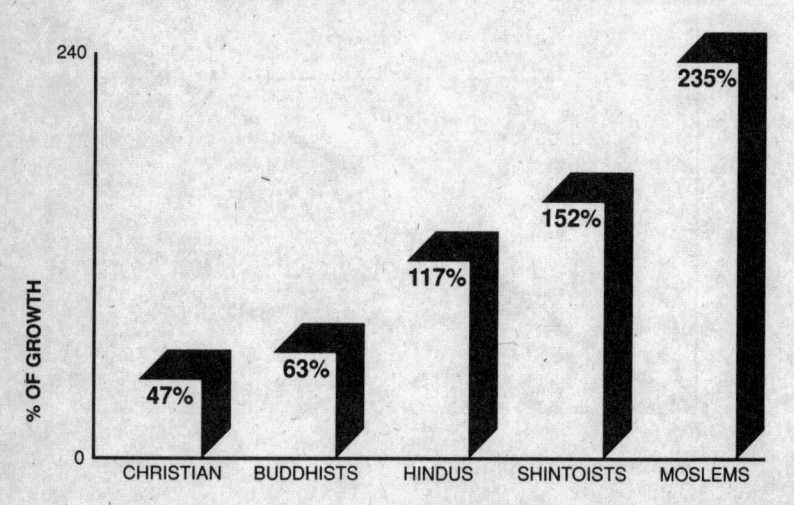

- CHRISTIAN: 47%
- BUDDHISTS: 63%
- HINDUS: 117%
- SHINTOISTS: 152%
- MOSLEMS: 235%

Appendix D: Charts on Factors Impacting Family Life 197

ISLAM EXCEEDS CHRISTIANS BY YEAR 2100

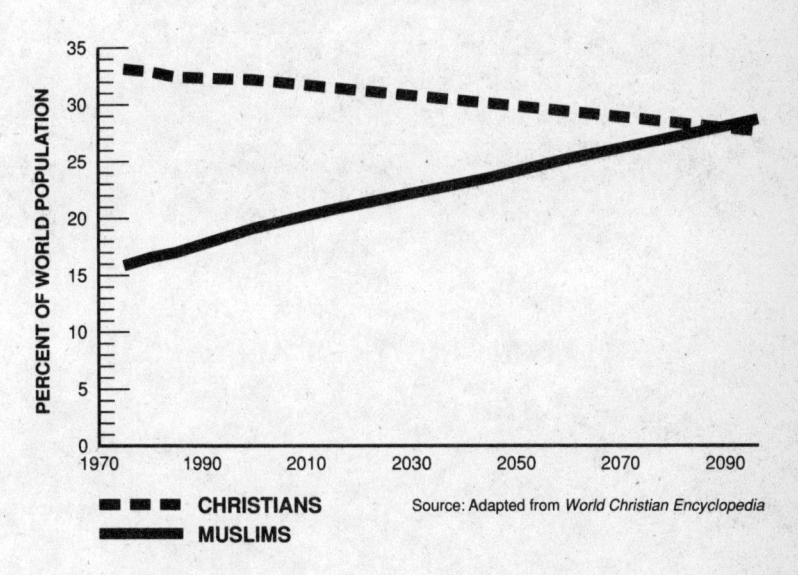

- - - CHRISTIANS
— MUSLIMS

Source: Adapted from *World Christian Encyclopedia*

APPENDIX E

Guiding Principles of Flourishing Family Life

A successful family is one which places its home under the authority of Jesus Christ, in which the husband is the head of the home and loves his wife as Christ loves the church, in which the wife is both helpmeet and homemaker, submitting to her husband as to the Lord, and in which the children are obedient to both. This is the God-given model.

Each of us has enough time to do what we were placed here to do. That must be our central focus—to work earnestly in fulfilling the purpose the Master has for us. Time efficiency will elude us as long as Jesus is not sitting on the throne of highest priority in our hearts.

Parents who want their children to develop strong academic excellence, moral strength of character, and a healthy self-respect, to be socially well-adjusted, and to build spiritual depth and appreciation should seriously consider home education or a private Christian school.

Day-care should be avoided at all costs. Young mothers should not seek full-time employment outside the home if a simple and modest home life that meets the basic necessities of the family is feasible without it.

As much as is humanly possible, Christian families will avoid television and other environments over which they have no control, especially those that display immoral activity or suggestions or are addictive in nature.

We must choose continually to avoid activities and environments where immorality is likely to be foisted upon us or our children.

If we are not content with what we have, we will not be content by obtaining more of what we do not have. We must seek our riches in Jesus Christ!

The Christian family will make its calling to be salt and light to others a top priority and a concern of urgent prayer.

As far as is possible and reasonable, Christian families must *insulate* themselves from ungodly cultural influence and activity without *isolating* themselves. Christians are called to witness and to warfare!

As God's people on earth, we must face the awful realities of our fallen society, choose to go beyond our excuses for non-involvement, and bravely lead the way in knowing and serving the God of Heaven.

Despite the difficulties and loneliness of radical Christianity, we must choose again and again to be faithful to the One who has called us to follow Him.

Rather than always choosing the road of ease and comfort, radical Christians keep following Christ, no matter what the cost!

True Christians serve Christ, not the crowd! Allegiance to the Master must be protected and renewed however and whenever necessary.

Radical Christians make a clear stand for the value of life and will do whatever God asks to fight the abortion holocaust and other such evils. This must be seen as all-out war against the spiritual forces of wickedness and must be fought in God's way and with God's weapons.

As radical Christians, it is imperative that we maintain an optimism and hope in the Lord, looking beyond the negativity of others and focusing on His purposes for us.

We must select and wear clothes that will not cause another man or woman to stumble. Could we wear these clothes before the Lord Jesus Christ without embarrassment?

To help our sons and daughters avoid lust and impurity, we must not allow them to go out alone with the opposite sex in unsupervised situations. We should help them avoid any setting or social environment that fosters or abets sin.

Radical Christian parents trust God to determine the size of their families and welcome children as special gifts from a loving Lord.

As committed Christians and as parents, we owe it to God to do His will and to clearly and fully choose *life*.

Radical Christianity is a lifelong walk in the will of God, and retirement years bring special opportunities we dare not ignore or squander.

Radical Christians are eager to honor a day which gives preeminence to worship, spiritual growth, physical rest, and the mutual uplifting of family members.

Does that particular book or magazine we are interested in edify? Can our families read it without being subjected to suggestive advertising? Does it contain material that could cause family members to stumble or will numb their sensitivity to righteousness?

In following the Lord Jesus Christ, we must be alert for opportunities to lead others into an increasing knowledge of God, to disciple them to the glory of God.

As parents and as committed Christians, we must reject any music which has anti-Christian content and must teach our sons and daughters to do the same. We must not only tell our children what music is wrong but why.

Radical Christians do not try to maintain a religious routine but rather allow God to reproduce the character of Christ in and through them day by day.

Serious Christians do not underestimate the importance of spiritual warfare in their homes, but rather fight the good fight, relying on the power, love, and wisdom of God.

The Christian family which truly follows Christ is ever on guard against temptation and moral compromise. This ought never to be taken lightly!

Effective world evangelization depends on families accepting a responsible role in winning the lost. Flourishing families will rediscover their place and purpose in the mission of God.

Refusing to take the easy way out, rejecting all rationalizations which excuse non-obedience to the Great Commission, radical Christian families are ready to serve the Master wherever and however He asks!

Committed Christian families will do all they can to be aware of missionary opportunities available to them and will trust God to show them which doors to walk through, for His glory.

Radical Christian parents see the importance of family zeal for missions, teach their children to win others to Christ, and help the family work together to serve the Lord as His witnesses.

NOTES

CHAPTER ONE: *The Challenge to Christian Families*

1. Between 1960 and 1984, the average tax rate for a couple with two children climbed 43 percent. For a couple with four children, the increase was an incredible 223 percent. Intentional or not, the nation's tax code has been penalizing families with dependent children. *The Family—Preserving America's Future*, November 1986, p. 60.
2. *Harpers Magazine*, "Harper's Index," October 1988, p. 15.
3. Zig Ziglar, *Raising Positive Kids in a Negative World* (Nashville: Thomas Nelson, 1985), p. 114.

CHAPTER TWO: *Assaults on the Family, Part I*

1. "U.S. Students Are Stumbling Through School," *USA Today*, September 27, 1990, p. 1D.
2. *Time*, January 23, 1984, p. 57.
3. *USA Today*, September 26, 1990, p. 3A.
4. Ray Ballmann, *The How and Why of Home Schooling* (Wheaton, IL: Crossway Books, 1987), p. 46.
5. *Focus on the Family Magazine*, "Who's Minding the Kids?," August 1988, p. 4.
6. *The Family In America*, "Day Care: Thalidomide of the 1980's?," November 1987, Vol. 1, No. 9, p. 5.
7. *Ibid.*, p. 2.
8. John Bowlby, *Child Care and the Growth of Love* (New York: Penguin Books, 1953), p. 11.
9. *Ibid.*
10. Policy paper on day-care, "Policy Concerns," published by Concerned Women For America, pp. 7, 8.
11. *Ibid.*, pp. 8, 9.
12. Shirley Samuels, *Enhancing Self-concept in Early Childhood* (New York: Human Science Press, 1977), p. 34.
13. "Who's Minding the Kids?," p. 3.
14. *Washington Post*, April 23, 1988.

15. "The Day-care Dilemma," *New Dimensions*, November 1990, Vol. 4, No. 11, pp. 26, 27.
16. *Ibid.*, p. 4.
17. "Policy Concerns," p. 7.
18. "Risk Factors for Hepatitis A in Day-care Centers," *Journal of Infectious Diseases*, February 1982, 145 (2), pp. 255-261.
19. "AIDS Tots Win City Okay for Day-care," *New York Post*, 1988, p. 22R.
20. "Day Care: Thalidomide of the 1980's?," p. 5.
21. "Hard Truths About Day Care," *Reader's Digest*, October 1988, p. 91.
22. *Newsweek*, August 20, 1984, p. 44.
23. *Fort Worth Star Telegram*, February 11, 1990, Sec. 1, Page 19.
24. "Day Care Regulation: Serving Children or Bureaucrats?," *USA Today*, May 1987, p. 65.
25. *Ibid.*, p. 66.
26. *Ibid.*
27. *Ibid.*, p. 6.
28. "Hard Truths About Day Care," p. 90.

CHAPTER THREE: *Assaults on the Family, Part II*

1. "A Report of the Working Group on the Family," *The Family—Preserving America's Future*, p. 41.
2. *Ibid.*
3. Bob Larson, *Family Issues* (Wheaton, IL: Tyndale House, 1986), p. 257.
4. *Ibid.*
5. Josh McDowell and Dick Day, *Why Wait?* (San Bernardino, CA: Here's Life, 1987) p. 40.
6. James Dobson, *The Impact of TV on Young Lives*, pamphlet (Pomona, CA: Focus on the Family, 1983), p. 3.

CHAPTER FOUR: *Families Following the Master*

1. "Let's Give Salt a Fair Shake," *Readers Digest*, November 1988, p. 17.

CHAPTER FIVE: *Faithful in a Fallen Culture*

1. George Arthur Buttrick, ed., *The Interpreter's Dictionary of the Bible*, Vol. 4 (New York: Abingdon Press, 1962), p. 104.
2. M. E. Unger, *Archaeology and the New Testament* (Grand Rapids, MI: Zondervan, 1962), pp. 319, 320.
3. "The Secularization of America," *Discipleship Journal*, May 1987, p. 43.
4. Mel and Norma Gabler, *What Are They Teaching Our Children?* (Wheaton, IL: Victor Books, 1985), p. 173.
5. Condensed from a suggestion sheet entitled "37 Things You Can Do to Get Involved," distributed by Focus on the Family, Pomona, CA.
6. Nancy Leigh DeMoss, exec. ed., *The Rebirth of America* (Arthur S. DeMoss Foundation, 1986), p. 212.
7. *Ibid.*, p. 213.

8. Charles Colson, *Kingdoms in Conflict* (Grand Rapids, MI: Zondervan, 1987), pp. 247-249.
9. *Ibid.*, p. 251.
10. *The Rebirth of America*, p. 197.
11. *Ibid.*

CHAPTER SIX: *Radical Christian Living, Part I*

1. Tom Hopkins, *The Official Guide to Success* (New York: Warner Books, 1982), p. 71.
2. *Ibid.*, p. 73.
3. Josh McDowell and Dick Day, *Why Wait?* (San Bernardino, CA: Here's Life, 1987), p. 79.
4. See, for example, Psalm 51:10; Proverbs 1:10; 23:31-33; Matthew 5:28; 15:19; 1 Corinthians 6:18, 19; Ephesians 4:29; 5:3, 4; 5:12; Philippians 4:8; 2 Timothy 2:22; 1 Peter 2:11.

CHAPTER SEVEN: *Radical Christian Living, Part II*

1. Germaine Greer, *Sex and Destiny: The Politics of Human Fertility* (New York: Harper and Row, 1984), p. 186.
2. Gunnar Kvale, *et al.*, "A Prospective Study of Reproductive Factors and Breast Cancer," *American Journal of Epidemiology* 126 (November 1987), pp. 830-840.
3. *Ibid.*
4. Jacqueline Kasun, *The War Against Population* (San Francisco: Ignatius Press, 1988), p. 37.
5. *Ibid.*, pp. 206, 207.
6. Ben J Wattenberg, *The Birth Dearth—What Happens When People in Free Countries Don't Have Enough Babies?* (New York: Pharos Books, 1987), pp. 37, 38.
7. "The Birth Dearth," *U.S. News and World Report*, June 22, 1987, p. 58.
8. *Ibid.*, p. 59.
9. *Ibid.*
10. "America's New Civil War," *U.S. News and World Report*, October 3, 1988, p. 25.
11. "Abortion: What Do the Statistics Reveal?," fact sheet published by National Right to Life.
12. Mary Pride, *The Way Home* (Wheaton, IL: Crossway Books, 1985), p. 80.
13. "Children's Perceptions of Last-Chance Parents: Some Implications of Current Trends Toward Late Childbearing," *Child Welfare*, Vol. 66, No. 3 (May-June), pp. 194-205.

CHAPTER EIGHT: *Radical Christian Living, Part III*

1. Richard P. Dickey, *Managing Contraceptive and Pill Patients* (Durant: Creative Informatics, Inc., 1987), pp. 100-103.
2. *Ibid.*, pp. 110-143.
3. *Ibid.*, p. 135.

4. "Study Backs Pill's Ties to Breast Cancer," *USA Today*, October 2, 1990, p. 1A.
5. Elizabeth Connell and Howard Tatum, *Reproductive Health Care Manual* (Durant: Creative Informatics, Inc., 1986), p. 99, 100.
6. *Ibid.*, p. 111.
7. Robert Morris and Scott Bass, *Retirement Reconsidered* (New York: Springer Publishing Co., 1988), p. 6.

CHAPTER NINE: Radical Christian Living, Part IV

1. Robert Coleman, *The Master Plan of Evangelism* (Old Tappan, NJ: Fleming H. Revell), pp. 33, 41, 43.
2. In this regard, read Proverbs 13:10, 14, 18, 20; 15:31; 20:5; 24:26; 27:17; Romans 12:10, 11; 1 Thessalonians 2:18.
3. "Rockin' Rodents Lose Their Way," *The Evangelical Methodist*, Vol. 68, No. 3 (March 1989), p. 8.
4. *Ibid.*, pp. 102, 103.
5. R. C. H. Lenski, *The Interpretation of St. Paul's Epistles to the Philippians* (Columbus, OH: Wartburg Press, 1946), p. 797.

CHAPTER TEN: What? My Family Missionaries?

1. Keith Green, "The Call of the Lord," Last Days, #43.
2. Isaiah 66:24; Matthew 8:12; 13:50; Mark 9:43, 44, 48; Luke 16:23, 24; Romans 2:9; Revelation 14:11; 20:10.
3. George W. Peters, *A Biblical Theology of Missions* (Chicago: Moody Press, 1975), p. 328.
4. *Spurgeon's Expository Encyclopedia*, Vol. XI (Grand Rapids, MI: Baker, 1978), p. 104.
5. W. G. Polack, *The Handbook to the Lutheran Hymnal* (Saint Louis: Concordia, 1975), pp. 346, 347.
6. *Ibid.*, pp. 40, 41.
7. Green, "The Call of the Lord."
8. Bill Bright, *Teachers Manual for Ten Basic Steps Toward Christian Maturity* (San Bernardino, CA: Here's Life, 1982), p. 5.
9. James S. Stewart, *Thine Is the Kingdom* (Edinburgh: St. Andrew Press, 1956), pp. 14, 15.
10. Bright, *Teachers Manual for Ten Basic Steps Toward Christian Maturity*, p. 5.
11. Michael Green, *Evangelism in the Early Church* (Grand Rapids, MI: Eerdmans, 1970), p. 173.
12. Keith Green, "The Most Commonly Heard Excuses," Last Days, #43.
13. *The Great Commission Handbook* (SMS Publications, Inc., 1988), p. 13.
14. Daniel Bacon, *Who Me? A Missionary?* (Singapore: OMF, 1985), p. 22.
15. J. Herbert Kane, "Why I Believe in Foreign Missions," in *The Great Commission Handbook*, p. 16.
16. *Ibid.*
17. Bacon, *Who Me? A Missionary?*, p. 20.
18. Keith Green, "The Call of the Lord."

Notes

19. Michael Green, "*Evangelism in the Early Church*, p. 13.
20. Matthew 6:33.

CHAPTER ELEVEN: *Mission Options for Your Family*

1. "Serving the New Surge of Missions Candidates," *The Great Commission Handbook*, p. 18.
2. "Youth With A Mission Is People," YWAM pamphlet.
3. "So You Think God Has Called You to the Mission Field," STEM pamphlet.
4. Ronald Iwasko, "Tentmaking," *Mountain Movers*, November 1988, p. 10.
5. Freda Lindsay, "Evangelize the World Now," *Christ for the Nations Magazine*, Vol. 43, No. 7 (October 1990), p. 3.
6. "A Look at the Mormon Mission Effort—From the Inside," *World Christian* magazine, June-August 1985, pp. 30-33.
7. Stephen F. Olford, *The Secret of Soul-winning* (Chicago: Moody Press, 1963), p. 44.
8. Robert E. Coleman, *The Master Plan of Evangelism* (Old Tappan, NJ: Fleming Revell, 1963), pp. 106, 107.

CHAPTER TWELVE: *The Essence of a Flourishing Family*

1. Franky Schaeffer, *Bad News for Modern Man* (Wheaton, IL: Crossway Books, 1984), pp. 141, 142.

SCRIPTURE INDEX

Genesis

1:28	92, 100
3:1-6	127
9:1	92

Exodus

1:15-21	69
1:22—2:10	69
20:8	108

Numbers

11:11, 12, 15	65

Judges

8:24-27	125

2 Chronicles

28:19	57

Job

6:6	48

Psalm

90:12	163
112:2	101
127	92
127:3-5	92

Proverbs

4:23	37
8:13	55
13:10, 14, 18, 20	206
13:20	79
14:28	96
14:34	57
15:31	206
20:5	206
24:11, 12	71
24:26	206
27:12	127
27:17	206
28:15	57
29:2	58

Isaiah

5:1-7	157
6:8	131
55:10, 11	158
58:13, 14	110
66:24	206

Jeremiah

17:9	127

Daniel

3:13-18	69
6:26	55

Hosea

8:4 — 57

Matthew

2:7-12 — 69
4:6 — 127
5:10-12 — 67
5:13-16 — 45, 123
5:16 — 49
6:21 — 43
6:33 — 207
7:14 — 67
8:12 — 131, 206
9:37, 38 — 156
10:16 — 56
10:34 — 64
10:35-37 — 47
12:1-8 — 110
12:30 — 75
13:50 — 206
16:18 — 75
25:41 — 127
26:41 — 126
28:19 — 133, 138
28:19, 20 — 157

Mark

2:17 — 53
3:1-6 — 110
4:8 — 159
5:9 — 127
8:34, 35 — 144
9:43, 44, 48 — 206
9:48 — 131
10:29, 30 — 66
16:15 — 138
16:16 — 131

Luke

2:49 — 153
6:6-11 — 69
6:22 — 46
9 — 47
9:59, 60 — 141
9:61, 62 — 47

14:25 — 64
15 — 40
15:4, 7 — 132
16:23, 24 — 206
19:10 — 137
19:13 — 55

John

9:4 — 142
9:13-16 — 69
12:31 — 127
15:1-17 — 160
15:2 — 160
15:5, 8 — 160
15:8 — 157
15:12, 13 — 73
15:16 — 160
15:18, 19 — 46
15:20 — 66

Acts

1:8 — 138
4:19, 20 — 69
5:29 — 69
8 — 138
17:16ff. — 53

Romans

2:9 — 206
3:28 — 122
4:5 — 122
6:1-23 — 123
7:4 — 157
7:18-23 — 125
7:24 — 127
10:14 — 142
12:1, 2 — 124
12:10, 11 — 206
13 — 63
13:1-7 — 69
13:14 — 89
15:20 — 137

1 Corinthians

3:13, 14 — 157

Scripture Index

5:9-11	54
6:19, 20	157
10:12	126
10:14	142
10:23	112

2 Corinthians

1:5-7	123
2:16	49
4:7	123
6:14, 15	87
10:5	36
11:14	127

Galatians

2:16	122
5:16	41
5:22, 23	41, 47, 93

Ephesians

2:8, 9	122
2:10	123
5:3	82
6:5	124

Philippians

2:12	124
2:16	124
3:9	122
4:8	80

Colossians

2:16ff.	108

1 Thessalonians

2:18	206
5:22	82, 128

1 Timothy

1:18-20	123

2:15	101
5:14	92

2 Timothy

2:16-18	123
2:22	84
3:12	67

Titus

2:12-14	123

Hebrews

10:31	131
12:1-3	165
13:16	123

James

1:14	126
1:27	41
2:14-26	123

1 Peter

1:8	47
2:12	123
3:1, 2	123
3:3, 4	88
4:14	66
5:8	127

2 Peter

3:17	126

1 John

3:7, 10	123
4:4	94

Revelation

3:15, 16	47
14:11	206
20:10	206

GENERAL INDEX

A Beka Correspondence School, 168
Abortion, 12, 13, 22, 36, 60, 62, 63, 68, 69, 71, 73, 74, 75, 99, 100, 103
Adam, 82, 91, 110
Adams, John Quincy, 58
Advanced Training Institute of America, 168
AIDS, 12, 21, 29, 39, 99, 100
Alcohol, abuse of, 20, 36, 85, 120
American Family Association, 60
Apollos, 118

Bacon, Daniel, 140
Ballmann, Ray E., 167
Barnabas, 118
Barnby, Joseph, 133
Belshazzar, 55
Belsky, Jay, 24, 25
Belz, Mark, 76
Benson Music, 79
Bird, Harvey, 121
Birth control, contraceptives, 22, 92, 94, 103, 104, 105
Birth Dearth, The (Ben J. Wattenberg), 97
Bonhoeffer, Dietrich, 43
Bonnke, Reinhard, 151, 152
Bowlby, John, 25
Burke, Edmund, 55

Calvert School, 168
Campolo, Tony, 120
Capital Report, The, 113
Carnegie, Dale, 79
"Cat's in the Cradle, The" (Harry Chapin), 18
Cavazos, Lauro, 21
Chapin, Harry, 18
Child abuse, 12, 30, 31

"Child Development" (Jay Belsky and Lawrence Steinberg), 24
Christian Action Council, 74
Christian Legal Society, 59
Christian Liberty Academy, 169
Christian schools, 23, 86
Citizen, 114
Civil disobedience, 53, 68, 69, 70, 71, 72, 73, 74
Clubhouse Magazine, 115
Coffin, Lee, 69
Coleman, Robert E., 119, 159
Colson, Charles, 69, 71, 76, 120
Communication, ix, 14, 35
Concerned Women for America, 59, 107
Conservative Digest, 113
Crown Magnetics, 153, 154
Cusher, Irvin, 99

Daniel, 55
Darius, 55
Dating, 83, 84, 85, 86, 89, 90, 126, 194
Day-care, 12, 15, 24, 25, 26, 27, 28, 29, 30, 31, 32, 93
Demski, Robert S., 121
Discipleship see *Mentoring*
Discipleship Journal, 114
"Disorder in Our Public Schools," 21
Divorce, 12
Dobson, James, 120
Dodd, Chris, 24
Dramatized Bible Cassettes, 115
Drugs, 20, 85, 120
Dwight, Timothy, 23

Eagle Forum, 59, 107
Ehrlich, Paul R., 95
Elijah, 118

213

Elisha, 118
Engstrom, Ted W., 119, 120
Esther, 55
Eve, 91
Everyone Is Not Doing It!, 88

Fallows, Deborah, 30
Family in America, 114
Family planning/family size, 22, 91, 92, 101, 102
Felice, Francis P., 95
Feminism, feminists, 13, 15, 24, 91, 100, 101
Fernandez, Joseph, 22
Fine Art of Mentoring, The (Ted W. Engstrom), 119
Flinn, Chester E., Jr., 21
Focus on the Family, 114
Foundation for Family Development, 167, 171, 172
Frontline Communications, 153

Gideon, 125
God's Word Publications, 111
God's World Today, 115
Go Manual, The, 134
Great Commission, the, 70, 129, 137, 141, 142, 144, 152
Green, Keith, 138
Green, Michael, 142

Hadler, Stephen, 28
Hale, Everett, 57
Haskins, Ron, 30
Hewitt-Moore Child Development Center, 169
Hilkiah and Shaphan, 55
Hitler, Adolf, 58, 63
Home schooling, home education, 23, 86
Home School Legal Defense Association, 168
Hopkins, Tom, 80
Hosanna Kids' Praise, 116
How and Why of Home Schooling, The (Ray E. Ballmann), 167
Human Events, 113
Humanists, humanism, 12, 23, 49, 53, 62, 67, 100, 128

Immorality see *Sexual morality/immorality*
Integrity's Hosanna! Music, 79
Intercristo, 107, 150, 151
Istre, Gregory, 28

Jefferson, Thomas, 58, 62

Johnstone, Patrick, 156
John, the Apostle, 69, 70
John the Baptist, 55
Joseph, 55, 84, 124
Joshua, 118, 139
Josiah, 55

Kane, Herbert, 139
Kasun, Jacqueline, 96
Kemp, Jack, 97
Kennedy, John, 58
Kids' Praise, 116
Kingdoms in Conflict (Charles Colson), 76
Koop, Everett, 21

Larson, Bruce, 120
Latch-key children, 15, 24
Levine, Edward, 26
"Life chains," 62
Light of the world, 45, 46, 49, 50, 54, 94, 129, 163
Lord's Day, the, Sunday, 108, 109, 110
Lot, 125
Louisiana Pro-life Law, 75
Luther, Martin, 72

McDowell, Josh, 88
McGavran, Donald, 134
McMartin, Virginia, 30
Magi, the, 69
Maranatha! Music, 79
Maslow and Felker, 27
Master Plan of Evangelism, The (Robert E. Coleman), 119
Materialism, 14, 41, 42, 43, 53, 94
Media, the, 12, 24, 56
Mentoring, discipling, 44, 117, 118, 119, 120, 132, 141, 159
Miller, Brent, 83
Missions, and the family, 43, 107, 129 (Chapter 10 *passim*), 145 (Chapter 11 *passim*)
    short-term, 145, 146, 147, 148, 149, 152, 154, 156, 173 (Appendix C *passim*)
Modesty/immodesty, 21, 81, 82, 88
Moody Monthly, 113
Moses, 65, 69, 118
Mother's Work, A (Deborah Fallows), 30
Mountain Movers, 114
Music, 120, 121, 122

Nagera, Humberto, 26
Naomi, 118

General Index

National Center for Home Education, 167
National Coalition Against Pornography (NCAP), 60
National Legal Foundation, 59, 107
National Review, 113
Nebuchadnezzar, 55, 69, 70, 110
Nehemiah, 55
Netcong, 52
New Dimensions, 113
New Hope Press, 153
New Horizons, 11
Nixon, Richard, 69
Noah, 92, 94

Olford, Stephen, 159
Olsen, Terrence, 83
Operation Rescue, 71, 72
Operation Rescue, 60
Operation World (Patrick Johnstone), 156

Parenting, 101
    fatherhood, 12, 14, 88, 94
    motherhood, 14, 15, 26, 33, 88, 94
Parent's Guide to the First Three Years, A (Burton White), 32
Paul, 53, 80, 84, 101, 118, 123, 125, 126, 127, 137, 145, 149
Peer pressure, 12, 20, 68, 86
Peter, 47, 69, 70, 126, 127
Peters, George, 132
Phyllis Schlafly Report, 114
Planned Parenthood, 22, 95
Please Let Me Live, 62
Population Bomb, The (Paul R. Ehrlich), 95
Pornography, 56, 60, 61
Prayer, 14, 50, 55, 56, 62, 71, 73, 74, 75, 87, 89, 118, 122, 126, 138, 141, 145, 156, 158
President's Council, 59
Pride, Mary, 100
Priorities, ix, 18, 43, 45, 46, 47, 50, 69, 72, 111, 163
Priscilla and Aquila, 118
Project Respect, 88
Public education, public schools, 12, 20, 21, 22, 23, 38, 72

Readers Digest, 113
Reading, value of good, 111, 112, 115, 153
Reagan, Ronald, ix, 21
Reap Resources, 61
Retirement, 14, 105, 106, 107, 108
Right To Life, 61
Robertson, Pat, 97

Roe v. Wade, 52, 73, 74, 75
Roles, family, 13, 14, 15, 16
Roman Empire, 51, 52, 53, 68
Ruth, 118
Rutherford Institute, 59, 107

Saturday Evening Post, 113
Salt of the earth, 45, 46, 48, 49, 50, 54, 62, 67, 75, 81, 94, 165
Samson, 86, 125
Schaeffer, Franky, 164
Schempp v. Murray, 52
School-based clinics, 22
Schreckenberg, Gervasia, 121
Seton Home Study School, 169
Sexual morality/immorality, ix, 12, 21, 22, 37, 38, 39, 40, 41, 61, 82, 83
Shadrach, Meshach and Abednego, 69, 70
Shaver, John, 31
Short Term Evangelical Missions (STEM), 146, 147
Silent Scream, The, 60
Smith, Oswald, 141
Solomon, 92, 125, 127
Souter, David, 75
Spurgeon, C. H., 84, 133
Steinberg, Lawrence, 24
Stephen, 138
Stepping Out, 148
Stewart, James, 136
STL Publications, 156
Suffer the Little Children (Mark Belz), 76
Summit Christian Academy, 169
Swindoll, Charles, 120
Sycamore Tree, The, 169

Teaching Home, The, 168
Teen Aid, 88
Teen Missions International, 154
Television, 13, 15, 16, 18, 35, 36, 37, 38, 42, 80, 81, 109, 111, 117, 143
ten Boom, Corrie, 69
Tentmaking missionaries, 149, 150, 151, 152
Tentmakers International (TI), 150, 151
Timothy, 84, 118
Trocmé, André, 69

Underground Railroad, 69

Value clarification in public schools, 20, 23

War Against Population, The (Jacqueline Kasun), 96
Wattenberg, Ben J., 97, 98
Webster, Daniel, 63
Webster v. Reproductive Health Services, 74
Wee Sing Silly Songs, 116
White, Burton, 32
Whitehead, John, 72
Why Wait? (organization), 88
Why Wait? (Josh McDowell), 88
Winnable War, A, 60
Witness, evangelism, ix, 42, 43, 45, 53, 54, 82, 100, 117, 118, 119, 129, 130, 131, 132, 134, 135, 136, 137, 138, 143, 156, 157, 159, 164 see also *Missions, and the family*
Women's liberation movement, 13
Word Kids' Music Club, 115
World Christian Teams (WCT), 147
World Missions Book Club, 153

Youth With A Mission (YWAM), 146, 147

Zacchaeus, 53
Zigler, Edward, 32